GRANTCRAFT

The Practitioner's Guide to Strategic Funding for Public Service, Healthcare, and the Nonprofit Sector

David E. Fraser, Ed.D., MPA

Fraser Leadership Group

Copyright © 2025 by David E. Fraser
All rights reserved.

No part of this publication may be reproduced, distributed, or transmitted in any form or by any means, including photocopying, recording, or other electronic or mechanical methods, without the prior written permission of the publisher, except in the case of brief quotations embodied in critical reviews and certain other noncommercial uses permitted by copyright law.

First Edition
ISBN: 979-8-9996165-5-5
Published by Fraser Leadership Group
www.fraserleadership.com

Printed in the United States of America

*For the visionaries and change-makers
working tirelessly to serve their communities
with integrity, clarity, and heart.*

Foreword

In the dynamic and often challenging landscape of public administration, healthcare, and nonprofit service, the ability to translate vision into tangible impact is paramount. This requires not only dedication but also **practical skills** in resource acquisition and program development. It is within this critical context that Dr. David E. Fraser's new book, *Grantcraft: The Practitioner's Guide to Strategic Funding for Public Service, Healthcare, and the Nonprofit Sector*, emerges as an essential and truly transformative guide.

My own journey in public health and program leadership, deeply rooted in health education (Ed.D.), public health (MPH), and food science, has shown me the profound need for practical, ethical, and results-driven approaches to community health challenges. As a Director of Programs providing vital services for individuals with Intellectual and Developmental Disabilities, and having previously served as an adjunct professor in the Master of Science in Healthcare Administration program at California State University, East Bay, I consistently seek resources that bridge theory and practice. My experience with Contra Costa Health, particularly in developing an innovative pandemic program with community health ambassadors, further underscores my appreciation for effective, community-based interventions.

I have had the distinct privilege of witnessing Dr. Fraser's unique pedagogical approach firsthand, both as an attendee at his insightful workshops and as a guest lecturer in his classes. His ability to demystify complex concepts and empower professionals with actionable strategies is unparalleled. He doesn't just teach *what* to do, but *how* to think strategically, ethically, and impactfully in the pursuit of resources.

This book is a direct reflection of that transformative teaching philosophy. Dr. Fraser meticulously unpacks the grant-seeking process, offering a roadmap that is as comprehensive as it is accessible. For the nonprofit sector, in particular, where every dollar is hard-won and every program vital, this book is not merely a manual; it is a lifeline. It provides the clarity, structure, and ethical grounding necessary to navigate the competitive funding landscape and secure the resources needed to drive meaningful change.

Dr. Fraser's dual perspective—as both a seasoned grant applicant who has secured millions in funding and a meticulous reviewer—imbues every chapter with invaluable, real-world wisdom. He empowers readers to think like funders while writing as passionate advocates for their cause. I am confident that anyone involved in seeking support for critical public services, healthcare initiatives, or nonprofit missions will find this book to be an indispensable tool, transforming their approach to grant writing and significantly amplifying their capacity for impact.

Dr. Nicola Ifill, Ed.D., MPH, M.S.
Nonprofit Program Director
Former Adjunct Professor, California State University, East Bay

Preface

Grant writing: it's both an art and a rigorous discipline. After more than three decades as a public administrator, nonprofit executive, and professor, I've seen firsthand how this powerful tool, when wielded effectively, can bring bold ideas to life, transforming aspirational concepts into tangible programs, and unlock unprecedented opportunities for communities and causes that truly need them.

My dual experience as both a successful applicant—raising over $25 million in grants, contracts, and philanthropic support for a wide array of diverse initiatives, spanning critical public-sector projects, vital community nonprofit programs, academic research partnerships, and broad regional coalitions—and an evaluator for grant applications (including as vice-chair of a local mitigation fund committee) has granted me unique insights. I've learned that truly fundable proposals are never just informative; they are deeply **intentional**. They masterfully blend a logical framework with crystal-clear communication, demonstrating profound respect for the funder's mission while passionately articulating the applicant's vision.

My journey to writing this handbook began in 2005, when I had the privilege of joining the Department of Public Affairs & Administration at California State University, East Bay. I was initially invited to develop a summer elective graduate course in philanthropy and grant writing. Over the years, my role expanded to include a broad spectrum of courses, deepening my understanding of the practical challenges faced by professionals in public service. It was approximately ten years ago, as the department explored offering a Master of Science in Healthcare Administration, that I was invited to develop the specific course on program development, evaluation, and grant writing. Each year as I teach this course, I've consistently grappled with a significant challenge: finding current, comprehensive textbooks that truly contain all the relevant information—from foundational theory to actionable strategies—that both meet the rigorous academic needs of my graduate students and serve as a practical guide for seasoned practitioners in the field. This persistent struggle solidified my conviction that I had to, at some point, write a text that filled this critical gap—***Grantcraft: The Practitioner's Guide to Strategic Funding for Public Service, Healthcare, and the Nonprofit Sector***. This book is the direct result of that commitment.

Having taught nearly 6,000 graduate students over my academic career, my goal, whether in a classroom or a seminar hall, remains the same: to demystify grant writing and empower professionals to see it as a **tool**, not a daunting hurdle. In every course, I emphasize that while strong writing is essential, *truly* successful proposals are built on deeper foundations: unwavering mission clarity, robust partnerships, and highly realistic plans. Ultimately, I want my students and readers to internalize how to think strategically like experienced reviewers, while simultaneously writing with the passion and clarity of dedicated advocates for their cause.

One of my most memorable experiences came during an all-day seminar I taught in Antioch, California. A first-time grant writer, representing her local Animal Services agency, actively engaged with the material. She began outlining a proposal based on the very straightforward, actionable principles we discussed that day—principles covering compelling need, logical structure, measurable outcomes, and precise budget alignment. A few months later, she shared exhilarating news: her agency had been awarded over $250,000 in grant funding, applying the strategies she developed. Her excitement was palpable, and her message powerfully reminded me what's possible when intention and preparation meet opportunity.

This handbook aims to empower anyone seeking to become more confident and effective in the grant writing process. It is not a dense academic text, nor is it a formulaic workbook. Instead, it's a **structured, field-tested guide**, born from extensive experience and designed to walk you through the process step-by-step. You'll find practical tools, realistic examples, and candid insights throughout – not generic formulas, but a nuanced roadmap that genuinely reflects the unique realities of working in public service, healthcare, education, and community development—sectors where ambitious goals are often met with significant challenges, and where every resource must be maximized. These are spaces where the need is immense, resources are scarce, and **every single dollar has the power to transform lives.**

If you are holding this book, chances are you have a vision for your community, your agency, or your cause. You know what you want to do—but you need resources to do it. My hope is that this guide will help you translate your vision into a compelling proposal—and help you find your unique voice as a grant writer.

Finally, I wish to express my profound gratitude to those who have significantly shaped my professional journey and, by extension, the very essence of this book. I am deeply thankful to **Dr. Toni Fogarty**, Professor Emeritus at California State University, East Bay, who not only entrusted me with the opportunity to design a required course for the Master of Science in Healthcare Administration but also empowered me to focus it squarely on program development, evaluation, and grant writing—the very themes that anchor this text. My sincere appreciation also goes to **Dr. Jay Umeh**, Professor Emeritus at California State University, East Bay, whose collaborative spirit in both teaching and joint research was instrumental in honing my skills in program evaluation, a critical component of effective grant seeking. Lastly, I honor the memory of the **late Supervisor Federal D. Glover**, who many years ago extended a pivotal invitation to present the first all-day seminar on grant research, writing, and administration. That initial engagement, born from his vision, organically morphed into an annual presentation, directly shaping much of the practical guidance within these pages. Their trust, mentorship, and collaboration have been invaluable.

Table of Contents

FOREWORD I
PREFACE III
TABLE OF CONTENTS VI
INTRODUCTION IX
    My Philosophy of Grant Writing X
    How to Use This Book XII

CHAPTER 1: UNDERSTANDING GRANTMAKERS AND PHILANTHROPY 1
    1. Foundations 2
    2. Corporations and Corporate Giving Programs 4
    3. Government Agencies 5
    Current Trends and Disruptors in Philanthropy 5

CHAPTER 2: PREPARING TO WRITE A GRANT PROPOSAL 12
    Conducting a Feasibility Study: The "Should We Do This?" Question 12
    Case Example 1: A Cautionary Tale 15
    Case Example 2: A Prepared Approach 15
    Understanding Funder Guidelines and Priorities 17
    Getting Organizational Buy-In: Building a Winning Team 21

CHAPTER 3: ANATOMY OF A WINNING PROPOSAL 25
    Abstract 26
    Executive Summary 26
    Statement of Need: The Data-Driven Core of Your Proposal 28
    Goals, Objectives, Outcomes, and Impacts (GOII): Mapping Your Journey to Change 32
    Program Description and Methods: The "How" You'll Make a Difference 34
    Evaluation Plan: Proving Your Impact (Overview) 35
    Budget and Budget Narrative: The Financial Story (Overview) 37
    Sustainability Plan: Beyond the Grant Period 39
    Appendices and Supporting Documents: The "Proof" 40

CHAPTER 4: BUDGET DEVELOPMENT AND LOGIC MODELS 44
    Budgeting Basics and Foundational Concepts: The Language of Resources 44
    Common Budgeting Challenges and Practical Solutions 48

- Types of Grant Budgets: Adapting Your Financial Presentation 49
- Sources and Uses Budgeting: The Gold Standard for Transparency and Balance 54
- Logic Models: Visualizing Program Logic for Budget Development 59

CHAPTER 5: EVALUATION – DEMONSTRATING IMPACT AND MEASURING SUCCESS 66

- Why We Evaluate: Purpose and Use – Beyond Compliance 70
- Evaluation Design Types: What You Evaluate 71
- Evaluation Methodologies and Approaches: Gathering and Interpreting Data 76

CHAPTER 6: WRITING, REVISING, AND POLISHING YOUR PROPOSAL 86

- The Purpose of Proposal Writing: Persuasion with Purpose 86
- Typical Grant Proposal Components (and their interconnectedness): 88
- Tips for Structuring Your Narrative for Maximum Impact: 90
- Writing Techniques for Clarity and Impact: Crafting Compelling Prose 92
- Common Pitfalls and How to Avoid Them 95
- Tools and Resources for Writing and Revision 99

CHAPTER 7: SUBMISSION, GRANT MANAGEMENT, AND REPORTING 102

- The Critical Pre-Submission Checklist: 102
- Common Submission Pitfalls and Their Prevention: 103
- Post-Award Grant Management: What Happens After You Win 104
- Narrative and Financial Reporting: Telling the Story of Impact and Stewardship 108
- Grant Closeout and Sustainability: Ensuring Lasting Impact 112

CHAPTER 8: REAL-WORLD GRANT PROPOSALS – AN ILLUSTRATIVE ANALYSIS 116

CHAPTER 9: BEYOND THE APPLICATION — ETHICS, INTEGRITY, AND RESPONSIBILITY IN GRANT WRITING 129

- The Temptation to Overpromise: Realistic Goals, Credible Impact 130
- Copy-and-Paste Syndrome: The Perils of Uncritical Reuse 131
- Budgets That Stretch the Truth: Financial Integrity 133
- Authorship and Attribution: Ownership and Accountability 134

REFERENCES 138

APPENDIX A: GRANT FEASIBILITY STUDY WORKSHEET 139

APPENDIX B: LOGIC MODEL TEMPLATE AND SAMPLE	142
APPENDIX C: SAMPLE SOURCES AND USES BUDGET (DETAILED ALLOCATION)	143
APPENDIX D: BUDGET JUSTIFICATION CHECKLIST	145
APPENDIX E: EVALUATION PLANNING WORKSHEET	149
APPENDIX F: SAMPLE DATA COLLECTION PLAN	156
APPENDIX G: OUTCOMES MATRIX TEMPLATE	162
APPENDIX H: SAMPLE EVALUATION REPORT OUTLINE	166
APPENDIX I – SAMPLE PROPOSAL 1	172
APPENDIX J – SAMPLE PROPOSAL 2	198
GLOSSARY	220
ABOUT THE AUTHOR	243

Introduction

In the dynamic world of public administration, healthcare, and nonprofit management, the ability to secure grant funding isn't merely advantageous—it's **indispensable**. Today's grant landscape is more competitive and complex than ever before. Funders increasingly demand greater accountability, sharper outcomes, and measurable impact, all while thousands of dedicated organizations fiercely compete for a finite pool of funds. Recent data underscores this reality: the 2025 *State of Grantseeking* report reveals that a staggering **71% of organizations perceive a significant increase in funding competition** over the past three years, and 85% **report a growing demand for their services**, often with painfully limited resources to meet these pressing needs. Adding to this challenge, funders themselves are continually evolving their priorities, emphasizing more equitable, data-driven programming and rigorously tighter evaluation strategies.

For countless professionals, from city managers and public health directors to nonprofit executives and social services leaders, grant writing is no longer an occasional task; it has become an **essential competency**. Yet, surprisingly few receive formal, practical training in crafting proposals that are both strategically sound and truly fundable. This critical gap—between the urgent need for resources and the skills required to secure them—is precisely what this book aims to bridge.

Why This Book and Why Now

This handbook was specifically crafted for the dedicated professionals navigating today's complex civic and service ecosystems. Whether you're a seasoned public sector administrator, an aspiring nonprofit or healthcare executive, a graduate student charting your career path, or a vital member of a program staff, this book is designed to help you become a stronger, more confident, and ultimately more effective grant writer. Beyond individual growth, it also serves as an invaluable resource for faculty, instructors, team leads, and consultants seeking a practical, real-world tool to guide staff or students through the intricacies of grant development.

Unlike theoretical academic texts focused on philanthropic history or abstract fundraising models, this book offers a **field-tested, application-first guide**. It cuts through the jargon, providing clear, actionable steps designed to mirror what today's funders truly expect. To ensure maximum utility and accessibility for busy professionals, the foundational research and best practices cited throughout these pages are predominantly drawn from publicly available reports, reputable organizational guidelines, and established, open-access academic resources, rather than paywalled journals. This intentional approach ensures that readers can easily explore and verify the evidence underpinning our strategies. We'll walk you sequentially through the entire lifecycle of a grant proposal: from precisely identifying a community need and shaping a compelling program concept, to meticulously aligning with funder priorities, developing a persuasive narrative that resonates, and diligently preparing for crucial post-award management and reporting. It's built for both new grant writers seeking a clear roadmap and experienced professionals who want to refine their approach with cutting-edge strategies, proven formats, and efficient workflows.

For the often-time-constrained professional—especially executives in nonprofit agencies, government departments, and healthcare institutions—this book offers more than just instruction; it's a **quick-reference resource** designed for immediate utility. Its user-friendly, modular structure allows you to consult relevant sections based on your immediate needs, without the obligation of reading cover-to-cover. This adaptability makes it an equally valuable companion for busy leaders needing quick answers, emerging grant writers building foundational skills, and dynamic teams collaborating on complex proposal development efforts. In essence, it's designed to fit seamlessly into the fast-paced realities of your professional life, delivering targeted guidance precisely when you need it most.

My Philosophy of Grant Writing

Over the course of my career, I've had the distinct privilege of engaging with hundreds of grant proposals from every angle—as a practitioner passionately pursuing resources, as an instructor guiding aspiring professionals, and as an evaluator rigorously assessing applications. Through this multifaceted experience, one lesson stands out above all: **grant writing is not merely technical writing; it is strategic storytelling.** When executed well, a grant proposal doesn't just inform; it weaves a clear, persuasive, and evidence-based narrative about *why* a project profoundly matters, *how* it will be meticulously executed, and what tangible, lasting impact it will deliver to the community. It's a delicate balance of art and discipline, much like the practice itself.

To me, grant writing is also a powerful form of **advocacy**. It's the vital channel through which organizations communicate with those who hold the purse strings, articulating not just a request, but a compelling case: "Here's why our community matters. Here's how we can make a measurable difference—if we have the resources to do it." This guide wholeheartedly encourages you to adopt that transformative mindset: to write always with unwavering mission, crystal clarity, and measurable intention.

My overarching philosophy is built upon three interconnected pillars, each informed by invaluable insights gained from decades spent on both sides of the funding equation—submitting proposals, managing awards, and meticulously evaluating applications:

- **Strategic Vision:** This emphasizes the crucial process of aligning a well-researched, deeply understood problem with a truly fundable solution. It demands a clear vision of measurable outcomes and an unwavering commitment to aligning with the specific priorities of potential funders. This pillar focuses on *what* you propose and *why* it fits.

- **Empathetic Communication:** This involves more than just eloquent prose. It's about writing with profound clarity, developing a fluid narrative flow, and injecting genuine emotional resonance, all while keenly recognizing and respecting the funder's unique constraints, values, and strategic goals. This pillar focuses on *how* you tell your story.

- **Accountable Stewardship:** At its core, this is about treating grant funding not just as a financial award, but as a profound public trust. It requires demonstrating rigorous operational readiness, showcasing sound and transparent budgeting, and maintaining a robust, verifiable track record for delivering tangible impact and unwavering transparency. This pillar focuses on *how* you manage and report.

How to Use This Book

Each chapter in this book is thoughtfully designed to build sequentially, guiding you from initial concept development through to successful post-award implementation. While readers may choose to work through the chapters in order for a comprehensive learning experience, the modular design also allows you to jump directly to a specific section based on an immediate need or particular challenge you're facing. This flexibility makes it an ideal resource. For instructors and faculty, the full text can be readily adopted for graduate-level courses in public administration, nonprofit management, or healthcare leadership, offering a robust curriculum. Similarly, agency supervisors will find it an excellent tool for staff training, professional development workshops, or even as an essential onboarding resource for new team members.

You'll discover a wealth of **practical tools** integrated seamlessly throughout the chapters, with even more comprehensive resources provided in the appendices. These include a meticulously crafted Grant Feasibility Study Worksheet designed to help you rigorously assess your project's readiness (**Appendix A**), a customizable logic model template (**Appendix B**), a detailed sources and uses budget sample (**Appendix C**), and a full evaluation planning worksheet to ensure robust impact measurement (**Appendix E**). As invaluable real-world reference points for structure, tone, and content, we've also included two complete sample grant proposals, generously developed by graduate students and shared with their permission (**Appendix I and Appendix J**).

Whether you are working in a city department, a regional health system, or a small nonprofit, the ability to write a compelling, fundable proposal can dramatically improve your agency's capacity and your personal impact. And the sooner you develop this essential ability, the more confident and successful you'll become in translating vision into reality.

This book won't just teach you the mechanics of applying for grants; it will help you develop the strategic mindset, the foundational structure, and the effective habits that truly define successful grant writers.

Let's begin.

Chapter 1: Understanding Grantmakers and Philanthropy

Successfully securing grant funding begins with a foundational understanding of the philanthropic environment in which grantmakers operate. It's not enough to simply identify a potential funding source—effective grant writing demands a deep insight into how various funding organizations think, act, and strategically align their giving with broader values, priorities, and societal goals. This chapter will provide a foundational understanding of the historical roots of philanthropy in America —**not as a dense academic study, but as crucial context for truly understanding today's funders**—, meticulously categorize the major types of grantmakers you'll encounter, and underscore the critical importance of cultivating strategic, enduring relationships with funders. By the end of this chapter, you'll possess a robust framework for approaching potential partners with informed confidence.

The Historical and Philosophical Roots of American Philanthropy

While this book is fundamentally a practical, application-focused guide, a brief overview of American philanthropy's rich history is exceptionally useful. It helps us understand the underlying motivations, the nuanced language, and the enduring institutional structures that continue to influence modern grantmakers and shape their decision-making processes today.

Philanthropy in the United States boasts a complex and fascinating history, deeply rooted in both moral obligation and strategic social investment. The very word itself—derived from the Greek "philanthrōpía," meaning "love of mankind"—powerfully encapsulates the ethical impulse to deploy personal wealth for the greater public good. In colonial America, giving was largely decentralized and community-driven, often focused on religious charities, mutual aid societies, and informal neighbor-to-neighbor support, profoundly shaped by church communities and fraternal organizations.

The dramatic rise of industrial capitalism in the 19th and early 20th centuries, spearheaded by titans of industry like Andrew Carnegie and John D. Rockefeller, irrevocably ushered in the era of large-scale, institutionalized foundations. These industrialists amassed enormous, unprecedented fortunes and, often guided by a burgeoning philosophy of civic responsibility and social engineering, began to formalize and institutionalize their giving. Carnegie's (1889) seminal essay, *The Gospel of*

Wealth, served as a powerful manifesto, arguing that the rich possessed a moral duty to distribute their accumulated wealth in ways that proactively improved society, rather than simply passing it on through inheritance. His visionary perspective catalyzed a profound shift from simple charity to strategic, planned philanthropy: not just providing immediate relief, but making long-term investments designed to address root causes and foster systemic change.

This profound transformation—from spontaneous, reactive giving to structured, mission-driven, and often proactive philanthropy—continues to shape grantmaking paradigms today. As Maurrasse (2020) compellingly notes in *Philanthropy and Society*, contemporary philanthropy has become increasingly **professionalized, data-driven, and intensely focused on achieving measurable systems change** rather than merely providing isolated service delivery. Modern funders, in turn, expect a high degree of alignment with their meticulously defined goals, demonstrable and measurable impact, and often robust, long-term sustainability plans from their potential grantees. This historical context underscores why today's grant proposals must be both strategically aligned and impact-oriented.

Types of Grantmakers

Modern grantmakers generally fall into three broad, yet distinct, categories: **foundations, corporations, and government agencies.** Understanding the fundamental differences among them—and their various subcategories—is absolutely critical to developing successful, targeted grant proposals.

1. Foundations

A **foundation** is a distinct legal organization, typically established as a nonprofit corporation or a charitable trust. Its fundamental purpose is to make financial grants to unrelated organizations or individuals for scientific, cultural, religious, educational, or other broadly charitable purposes. It's important to note the nuances here: charitable trusts described in Internal Revenue Code section 4947(a)(1) may not be tax-exempt themselves, but they are treated as private foundations for most purposes unless they meet specific exclusion criteria allowing them to be classified as public charities. As such, these charitable trusts are subject to private foundation excise tax provisions, termination requirements, and governing instrument rules. They are also subject to the excise tax on investment income under the rules that apply to taxable foundations, rather than the more lenient tax-exempt foundation rules. These distinctions are critical for understanding how foundations function within the broader philanthropic landscape and how they may or may not interact with grant-seeking organizations, particularly regarding transparency and reporting.

Foundations are legal entities specifically established to distribute funds for charitable purposes. They can be broadly categorized as:

- **Private Foundations:** These are typically funded by a single individual, family, or corporation (though corporate-funded ones are distinct from corporate giving programs, as we'll explore). They primarily make grants from an endowment, a substantial fund of money invested to provide annual income for charitable activities. Examples include the globally influential Ford Foundation, known for its work in social justice, and the Walton Family Foundation, deeply involved in environmental and education initiatives. Understanding their specific family history or corporate ties can often reveal their unique giving philosophies.

- **Community Foundations:** These are unique public charities that strategically pool resources from multiple donors, often individuals, families, and businesses, to serve a specific geographic area, be it a city, county, or region. They are governed by boards representing local communities, ensuring their grantmaking reflects local needs and priorities. Examples include the East Bay Community Foundation and the San Francisco Foundation, both of which play vital roles in addressing regional challenges through responsive grantmaking.

- **Operating Foundations:** Distinct from grantmaking foundations, these entities use most of their income and resources to directly run their own programs and initiatives, rather than primarily funding outside organizations. They are often deeply involved in research or direct service delivery. **A critical distinction for grant seekers: Unlike other foundations, operating foundations generally do not solicit or accept unsolicited grant applications.**

- **Caution:** Many aspiring grant writers mistakenly submit applications to operating foundations, unaware that these institutions do not typically accept unsolicited proposals, leading to wasted time and effort. Always verify a foundation's giving type before investing time in a proposal.

- **Public Foundations (or Public Charities that Grant):** While technically public charities, these organizations raise funds from the general public (e.g., through individual donations, events, or broader appeals) and often focus on specific missions such as biomedical research, environmental protection, or artistic endeavors. Because they rely on public support, they often engage more directly with the public and may have a broader range of grantmaking activities. Examples might include organizations like the American Cancer Society or the Environmental Defense Fund, which might operate programs but also issue grants related to their mission.

2. Corporations and Corporate Giving Programs

Corporate philanthropy generally takes two main, yet distinct, forms, each requiring a tailored approach:

- **Corporate Foundations:** These are legally distinct, separate non-profit entities funded by corporations but governed by their own independent boards. While connected to the parent company, they operate with a separate legal identity, often with more structured grant cycles and established priorities. The Coca-Cola Foundation, for example, operates globally, focusing on areas like water stewardship and community empowerment.

- **Corporate Giving Programs (or Corporate Social Responsibility - CSR Programs):** These programs operate directly through the corporation itself, integrated into its business operations. They can include direct cash gifts, often tied to marketing or brand-building initiatives, significant in-kind donations, or employee matching gift programs. Unlike foundations, they are not legally required to follow the same public reporting or payout rules, making their processes potentially less transparent but sometimes more flexible. Examples include Chevron's robust community investment arm and Apple's corporate responsibility programs.

Understanding whether a company gives through a formal corporate foundation or directly through a CSR program is **essential** to tailoring your proposal and outreach strategy. Corporate foundations may require formal applications and board review, while corporate giving programs may be more flexible but less transparent.

3. Government Agencies

Government grants come from federal, state, and local levels. These are often highly structured and guided by legislative or policy priorities.

- **Federal:** Agencies like the U.S. Department of Health and Human Services or Department of Education offer large-scale grants with rigorous application processes.
- **State and Local:** State health departments, housing agencies, or county offices often provide grants aligned with regional priorities. These may be more accessible to smaller organizations but still require accountability and performance tracking.

While government grants can be substantial, they are also complex, competitive, and compliance-heavy. Grant seekers must be prepared for detailed reporting, evaluation, and audit requirements.

Building Strategic Relationships with Funders

Grant seeking is not purely transactional—it is deeply **relational**. Establishing and nurturing relationships with funders increases credibility, visibility, and the likelihood of funding (Salamon, 2012).

Effective strategies include:

- Attending funder briefings, bidder's conferences, and grantor-hosted informational events—even before applying.
- Sending regular updates or annual reports to key funders.
- Inviting potential funders to visit your programs.
- Starting with smaller grants to build trust before seeking larger awards.

My research and extensive experience suggest that applicants without a prior relationship to a funder may have less than a 10% chance of receiving a grant. Early engagement and demonstrating alignment with a funder's mission are vital.

Current Trends and Disruptors in Philanthropy

Modern philanthropy continues to evolve in response to profound economic, social, and political pressures. Staying abreast of these shifts is crucial for successful grant seeking. Recent years have seen several transformative trends:

- **Equity-Focused Giving (DEI):** There's been a significant and growing emphasis on Diversity, Equity, and Inclusion (DEI) in grantmaking. Many funders are now explicitly prioritizing organizations that demonstrate a deep commitment to DEI within their own structures and programs. This includes actively supporting BIPOC-led (Black, Indigenous, and People of Color-led) organizations, channeling funds to grassroots initiatives often overlooked by traditional philanthropy, and intentionally prioritizing communities historically excluded from mainstream funding streams. Grant proposals that articulate a clear DEI lens in their program design and operations are increasingly favored. However, it's vital for grant seekers to recognize that this emphasis can vary significantly across funder types, particularly within the federal landscape. While many private and community foundations have largely sustained or even deepened their focus on DEI initiatives, federal grant programs, influenced by evolving administrative directives and legislative climates, may exhibit a more nuanced or at times, tempered approach to explicitly equity-focused criteria. This necessitates careful, up-to-date review of specific agency guidelines and funding opportunity announcements, as priorities can shift with changes in political leadership.

- **Trust-Based Philanthropy:** This is a rapidly gaining movement that fundamentally reimagines the funder-grantee relationship. It advocates for multi-year, unrestricted general operating grants, significantly streamlined application and reporting requirements, and building mutual respect between funders and grantees. It reflects a shift away from transactional funding models and toward deeper partnerships focused on long-term impact.

- **Critiques of Traditional Philanthropy:** Simultaneously, scholarly and public critiques of large-scale philanthropy have grown louder. Observers point out that vast philanthropic wealth can sometimes inadvertently reinforce existing societal inequities, promote top-down agendas that don't originate from community needs, or allow billionaires to influence public policy without corresponding democratic accountability. This heightened scrutiny has led to increased interest in greater transparency, genuinely participatory grantmaking, and democratizing access to capital (Murray et al., 2016).

- **Venture Philanthropy** and **Social Impact Investing:** Borrowing strategies from the business world, these innovative models are also on the rise. **Venture philanthropy** often focuses on high-impact, scalable solutions, with a strong emphasis on return on investment (social ROI), rigorous metrics, and the potential for an initiative to be replicated or grown. **Social impact investing** goes a step further, deploying capital (loans, equity, or hybrid instruments) to generate both financial returns and measurable social or environmental impact. While sometimes controversial due to their business-centric approach, they represent a growing portion of philanthropic capital, especially among younger donors, tech philanthropists, and entrepreneurial foundations seeking systemic change.

Real-World Examples of Grantmakers and Impact

Understanding funder behavior isn't theoretical—it has profound, real-world implications for grant seekers and directly impacts strategy. Take the **Bill & Melinda Gates Foundation**, for example. With a global health and education focus, it provides large-scale grants that often require deep collaboration, research-driven models, and robust evaluation plans, reflecting their emphasis on evidence-based impact at scale (Bill & Melinda Gates Foundation, n.d.). In contrast, the **Robert Wood Johnson Foundation** champions health equity within the United States, frequently funding multi-sector partnerships, fostering local innovation, and supporting policy advocacy that addresses the social determinants of health.

More recently, **MacKenzie Scott's philanthropy** has disrupted traditional norms by providing large, unrestricted grants with minimal application processes and no ongoing reporting obligations. Her radical approach reflects a deep trust in nonprofit leaders and a rejection of the idea that rigorous oversight is always necessary.

At a smaller scale, community foundations like the **San Diego Foundation** exemplify place-based giving, offering competitive grant cycles precisely targeted to address acute local priorities, from homelessness to environmental conservation. Similarly, **corporate giving programs** such as Kaiser Permanente's Community Health Grants actively fund nonprofits whose missions align with the company's broader commitment to addressing social determinants of health within the communities they serve.

A particularly helpful case study highlights the power of visibility and indirect relationship-building: A small youth development nonprofit in Northern California received an unsolicited grant from a local community foundation after being nominated by a donor-advised fund holder who had attended one of their events. This funder had been deeply impressed by their work. This kind of unexpected opportunity powerfully underscores the importance of consistent visibility, impactful program delivery, and the organic relationship-building that can occur even when funders aren't actively soliciting proposals.

How to Research and Assess Potential Funders

Identifying and thoroughly assessing potential funders is a critical skill in the grant writing process. Leveraging the right tools and strategies can save countless hours and dramatically increase your chances of finding the perfect match.

Key resources for comprehensive funder research include:

- **Foundation Directory Online (Candid):** A searchable database of private and community foundations, including giving priorities, contacts, and past grantees.

- **Grants.gov:** The primary source for federal grant opportunities.

- **990 Finder (ProPublica or Candid):** Allows users to publicly examine IRS Form 990s, which all U.S. tax-exempt organizations (including foundations) are required to file annually. These forms are treasure troves of information, revealing a foundation's assets, revenue, detailed expenditure breakdowns, list of past grant recipients, funding ranges, and even their payout rates, offering transparent insights into their giving patterns.

When researching, look for:

- Mission alignment with your organization or project
- Geographic or population focus
- Typical grant amounts and funding cycles

- Openness to unsolicited proposals

Red flags during your research are crucial to identify. These include out-of-date websites, a complete lack of clear contact information for program officers, or explicit language that indicates they only fund pre-selected organizations or through referral. Pursuing these can be a drain on limited organizational capacity.

Funders at a Glance: Comparison Table

Funder Type	Key Features	Application Style	Typical Considerations for Grant Seekers
Private Foundations	Endowment-based, often family or individual legacy; specific, sometimes narrow focus.	Formal, highly competitive; often accept Letters of Inquiry (LOIs) first.	Research specific giving interests, board members, and past grantees. Relationships can be key.
Public/Community Foundations	Local focus, pooled funds, open cycles	Community-based, public; typically open, competitive cycles; often focused on local impact.	Understand local priorities, engage with community stakeholders, demonstrate local impact.
Operating Foundations	Primarily run their *own* programs and initiatives; generally do *not* make grants to outside organizations.	Rarely applicable; generally do not accept external proposals.	**Caution: Do not apply unless explicitly invited or you understand their specific model.**
Corporate Foundations	Legally separate, board-governed entities funded by a corporation; often align with corporate values.	Programmatic alignment; often structured, with specific focus areas related to the company's business or values.	Research corporate mission, CSR reports, and their business footprint.

Funder Type	Key Features	Application Style	Typical Considerations for Grant Seekers
CSR Giving Programs	Direct corporate giving (cash, in-kind, employee matching); integrated into business operations.	Relationship-driven; often less formal, may be by invitation, or through employee referral.	Focus on mutual benefit, brand alignment, and local presence where the company operates.
Government Agencies	Public funds, compliance-heavy, structured applications	Highly formal, regulated; rigorous RFPs, detailed compliance, extensive reporting.	Requires strong project management, data collection, and financial systems. High competition.

Reflective Activity: Who Are Your Ideal Funders?

To effectively apply the insights from this chapter, take time for a critical self-assessment. Use the questions below to clarify the types of funders most likely to support your work:

- What is your organization's core mission?
- What specific geographic area or population do you primarily serve?
- What type of financial support do you most critically need (e.g., programmatic, capital, general operating)?
- Are you seeking small startup grants or large multi-year investments?
- Do you have the capacity to meet government reporting standards, or are you better suited for private or community foundations?

Create a concise shortlist of 5–7 funders whose values and focus areas closely align with your mission. Review their websites, guidelines, and previous grantees before reaching out or applying.

Conclusion

Understanding the historical evolution of philanthropy and the nuanced characteristics of various grantmakers is not just academic; it is absolutely essential for strategically navigating the modern grant funding landscape. By learning to intelligently differentiate between funder types, meticulously aligning your proposals with their distinct priorities, and proactively building strong, authentic relationships, grant seekers dramatically improve their chances of success—and ultimately increase their organization's capacity to serve.

Chapter 2: Preparing to Write a Grant Proposal

The most common mistake made by new, and even many experienced, grant writers is **starting too soon**. The understandable impulse to dive directly into writing—crafting compelling narratives and detailed budgets—without first thoroughly checking for organizational readiness or ensuring meticulous funder alignment can lead to profound frustration, wasted effort, and, most critically, a high likelihood of unfunded proposals. In this pivotal chapter, we will shift our focus entirely to what absolutely must come first: **strategic and comprehensive preparation.**

Whether you are embarking on your very first grant application or leading a seasoned grant team, deeply understanding your organizational readiness, rigorously evaluating a project's feasibility, acutely interpreting a funder's nuanced priorities, and securing robust internal alignment are not merely suggestions; they are **essential, non-negotiable first steps** that lay the groundwork for success. Skipping these initial stages is akin to building a house without a proper foundation—it may look good on the surface, but it's prone to collapse under pressure.

Conducting a Feasibility Study: The "Should We Do This?" Question

A grant proposal is far more than just a pitch for funding; it represents a significant commitment—a public promise to deliver on specific outcomes, manage resources responsibly, and contribute to a shared vision. Before your organization makes that commitment, it is absolutely imperative to ensure you are thoroughly prepared and equipped to follow through. The feasibility process is your crucial internal audit, asking fundamental questions: **Can we genuinely do this? Should we commit our resources to this endeavor? And, perhaps most importantly, should we do this *now*?**

A proper feasibility review is not merely a formality; it's a strategic deep dive into your organization's capacity and the project's viability. It typically includes an honest assessment across several critical dimensions:

- **Organizational Capacity:** This is an internal check on whether you possess the necessary human resources, administrative infrastructure, and unwavering leadership support to not only undertake but successfully deliver the proposed program.
    - *Depth:* Consider staff expertise and availability, existing technology and data systems, appropriate physical space, and the readiness of your financial systems to handle grant reporting and compliance. Does your current workload allow for this new initiative? Will additional training or hiring be required? Are key decision-makers fully on board and prepared to allocate internal resources?
- **Strategic Alignment:** This critical dimension asks if the proposed project is fundamentally consistent with your organization's established mission, values, and long-term strategic goals.
    - *Depth:* A project that doesn't align with your core mission can dilute your focus, strain resources, and send mixed messages to your stakeholders. Is this project an organic extension of your current work, or a departure? How does it contribute to your organization's vision for the future? A strong alignment ensures enthusiasm, consistent messaging, and organizational buy-in.
- **Community and Stakeholder Support:** True impact is rarely achieved in isolation. Have you genuinely engaged those who will be affected by or are essential to the project's success? This includes beneficiaries, community leaders, potential partners, and even local government officials.
    - *Depth:* Active involvement of stakeholders from the outset ensures the project addresses real needs, fosters a sense of ownership, and builds a coalition of support vital for implementation and sustainability. Are there existing community needs assessments that validate the problem your project seeks to address? Have you received letters of

support or Memoranda of Understanding (MOUs) from key partners?

- **Funder Fit:** This external assessment is about discerning if your project is genuinely aligned with the potential funder's stated priorities, their typical geographic focus, and their customary funding scale.

    o *Depth:* Does your project address one of their core programmatic areas (e.g., environmental justice, youth mentoring, accessible healthcare)? Do they fund in your specific city, county, or state? Do their typical grant amounts align with your project's budgetary needs? Applying to a funder whose interests are misaligned is a guaranteed path to rejection.

- **Evaluation and Sustainability:** Can you credibly measure the impact and outcomes of the proposed program? And, crucially, do you have a viable plan for sustaining the program beyond the initial grant period, or is this a one-time initiative?

    o *Depth:* Funders are increasingly focused on measurable results and long-term impact. An honest assessment here involves considering your data collection capabilities, identifying clear indicators of success, and brainstorming diverse funding streams or earned income strategies to ensure the project's continuation if it proves effective.

It's important to stress that conducting a feasibility study doesn't demand hiring an expensive formal consultant or launching a large-scale, months-long analysis. For most public administration, healthcare, and nonprofit organizations, a **structured internal review, meticulously guided by a worksheet** (see **Appendix A**: Grant Feasibility Study Worksheet), is perfectly sufficient. This internal process empowers your team to critically assess your readiness with minimal external cost.

Case Example 1: A Cautionary Tale

Consider the experience of a small health nonprofit that, driven by enthusiasm and urgency, once rushed to submit a proposal to a national foundation offering a substantial $250,000 in health equity funding. The core idea for a new community health outreach program was indeed promising and much needed in their service area. However, in their haste, the internal team hadn't formally secured letters of commitment from essential clinical partners, they lacked the necessary robust data systems to track participant outcomes, and, crucially, they had no clear strategy for how they would sustain the program once the initial grant funding inevitably ended. Predictably, the proposal was not funded. The invaluable feedback they received from the foundation explicitly highlighted the significant readiness gaps that could have been easily identified and addressed if they had simply paused for a comprehensive internal feasibility check before embarking on the writing process. This resulted in wasted staff time, a missed opportunity, and a minor setback to their credibility.

Case Example 2: A Prepared Approach

In stark contrast, a local workforce development agency situated in a mid-sized city demonstrated a prepared, strategic approach before applying for a competitive federal reentry grant. Rather than immediately drafting, they consciously invested time in an intensive internal review process. They formed a diverse, cross-functional planning team encompassing program, finance, and evaluation staff. They conducted preliminary meetings with local employers to gauge interest and secure job placement commitments, formalizing these with signed Memoranda of Understanding (MOUs). Furthermore, they meticulously confirmed their internal data tracking capacity to meet federal reporting requirements. While the application process undeniably took longer, the resulting proposal was exceptionally strong, logically structured, and demonstrated compelling readiness. Consequently, the proposal was approved, and the program not only met but significantly exceeded its stated outcomes, earning renewed funding in subsequent cycles. This case illustrates the tangible rewards of thorough preparation.

What If We're Not Ready? Strategic Adjustments and Smart Responses to Gaps

It is not uncommon, and indeed perfectly healthy, for a thorough feasibility study to reveal genuine gaps in readiness. This critical insight should never be interpreted as a sign to abandon a promising idea entirely. Instead, it serves as an invaluable roadmap, guiding you toward making **strategic adjustments** that strengthen your foundation and increase your chances of future success. Funders highly value self-aware organizations that understand their capacities. Rushing into a grant you are genuinely not ready to manage will almost always hurt your organization's long-term credibility far more than gracefully skipping a particular opportunity to build capacity first.

Smart and proactive responses to identified readiness gaps include:

- **Scale the Project Appropriately:** Instead of attempting to launch a sprawling, city-wide initiative immediately, consider scaling the project down to a more manageable scope. Start with one neighborhood, a smaller pilot population, or a single program component. This allows you to test your model, gather data, and build capacity incrementally. Many funders appreciate this realistic, phased approach.

- **Build Strategic Partnerships:** If your organization lacks certain expertise, infrastructure, or community connections, actively seek out and collaborate with experienced agencies or complementary organizations. By forming strong partnerships and clearly defining shared responsibilities (often formalized through MOUs), you can pool resources, share burdens, and leverage collective strengths to meet grant requirements.

- **Seek Planning or Capacity-Building Grants:** Recognize that not all grants are for program implementation. Many funders specifically support organizational development. Funders like the Robert Wood Johnson Foundation and various local community foundations often offer grants explicitly designed for needs assessments, developing robust evaluation frameworks, supporting pilot initiatives, or general organizational **capacity building** (e.g., improving IT infrastructure, staff training, strategic planning). These grants can help you address the very gaps your feasibility study identified.

- **Delay Until Ready: Timing Matters:** If a grant opportunity requires significant infrastructure, staffing, or data that you simply do not possess in the current moment, it is far wiser to delay your application until the next funding cycle. Use the intervening time to systematically build the missing components. Submitting a weak proposal just to meet a deadline is almost always counterproductive.

- **Start with an LOI or Concept Paper (if available):** Some funders offer a "lighter-touch" preliminary application format, such as a Letter of Inquiry (LOI) or a Concept Paper, before requiring a full proposal. Use these opportunities, if available, to gauge funder alignment and interest without investing extensive time in a full proposal. Positive feedback can then guide your capacity-building efforts.

Understanding Funder Guidelines and Priorities

Every funder, without exception, publishes some version of **guidelines** for their grant programs. These critical documents—which can range from concise online blurbs or short "Requests for Information" to highly detailed Requests for Proposals (RFPs) or Notices of Funding Opportunities (NOFOs) for government grants—outline not just basic eligibility and timelines, but also provide invaluable clues about the funder's deeper expectations, core values, and strategic priorities. Think of them as your grant-seeking compass.

What to look for, and meticulously analyze, within these guidelines:

- **Eligibility:** This is your absolute first filter. Are you the right type of organization (e.g., 501(c)(3) nonprofit, government agency, educational institution)? Are you located in the correct geographic area that the funder serves? Do you serve the specific population demographic they prioritize? Answering "no" to any of these immediately flags this as a non-fit.

- **Award Range and Duration:** Does the typical grant award amount align with your project's financial needs? Can you realistically deliver the proposed scope of work within their stated grant duration (e.g., 12 months, 24 months)? Applying for a $1 million project to a funder whose average grant is $25,000 is a waste of everyone's time.

- **Priority Areas and Programmatic Themes:** This is the heart of funder alignment. Does your work clearly and demonstrably align with their current thematic priorities (e.g., environmental justice, youth mentoring, accessible healthcare)? Look for keywords, phrases, and examples they use. Many funders list specific "program areas" or "focus issues."

- **Deliverables and Evaluation Requirements:** What specific outcomes or outputs does the funder expect? What kind of data and reporting will they require? Do you have the internal capacity, or a clear plan to develop it, to rigorously track progress, measure impact, and fulfill these reporting obligations? This often links back to your feasibility assessment.

Reading Between the Lines: Beyond the Explicit

Some funders are meticulously explicit about what they will fund and what they will not; others are more opaque, requiring a more nuanced interpretation. Here's how to go deeper and uncover implied priorities:

- **Review Past Grantees:** This is one of the most powerful research tools. Search the funder's website, examine their annual reports, or use public databases like IRS 990s (available via Candid's Foundation Directory Online or ProPublica's 990 Finder) to see who they've funded before. What types of organizations, projects, and geographic areas do their past awards demonstrate? Are there recurring themes or specific program models they consistently support?

- **Scan for Implied Priorities vs. Stated Goals:** A funder might state they are looking for "innovative" projects, but a review of their past grantees might show they primarily fund proven programs with incremental improvements. This indicates a preference for solid, reliable projects rather than truly experimental ones.

- **Pay Attention to Tone and Lexicon:** The language a funder uses in their guidelines and on their website provides subtle clues. A funder who heavily emphasizes "scalability" may be looking for programs that can be replicated or expanded to reach a wider audience, not niche interventions. One focusing on "systems change" is looking for projects that address root causes, not just symptoms.

- **Common Funderspeak—and What It Might Mean:** Understanding the common jargon used by grantmakers is like learning a new dialect. Here's a quick interpreter for frequently encountered terms:

Funder Language	What It Might Mean (and How to Respond)
"Innovative"	Don't just repeat your own past programs or common approaches; present something fresh, adapted, or a novel solution to an old problem. Showcase creativity while maintaining practicality.
"Evidence-based"	Ground your proposal in verifiable research. Cite peer-reviewed studies, established evaluation findings, best practices, or robust data that support your proposed interventions.
"Sustainability"	Have a clear, diversified plan beyond the grant. Don't rely on annual renewals.
"Equity-focused"	Demonstrate outreach to underserved populations or systemic barriers.
"Collaborative"	Show real partners with clear roles (not just letters of support).
"Capacity Building"	The funder is interested in strengthening your organization's infrastructure, skills, or ability to deliver, rather than directly funding a program. Be specific about the type of capacity you'll build.
"Measurable Outcomes"	Go beyond simply listing activities. Define clear, quantifiable results you expect to achieve and how you will track them.
"Leverage"	How will this grant multiply its impact? Show how it will unlock other resources, attract additional funding, or create broader systemic change.

Use these insights not just to tailor the language of your proposal, but fundamentally to **design your project** to align with the funder's deepest interests and expectations.

Getting Organizational Buy-In: Building a Winning Team

Strong, successful grant proposals are rarely the product of a single individual working in isolation; they are almost always **team efforts**. Before you even begin drafting the narrative, it is absolutely essential to assemble a dedicated grant team and secure the explicit, enthusiastic support of all involved departments and key stakeholders within your organization. This internal cohesion is as critical as external funder alignment.

Key internal stakeholders you must actively engage from the outset include:

- **Executive Leadership (CEO, Executive Director, Board Chair):** Confirm their explicit support for the overall project strategy, the proposed timeline, and the commitment of organizational resources (financial, staff, in-kind). They will likely be the final approvers and signatories, so their early and sustained buy-in is paramount.

- **Finance Department/CFO:** This is a non-negotiable partnership. Work closely with finance to review budget expectations, understand funder reporting requirements (e.g., quarterly financial reports, audit needs), and accurately calculate any required matching contributions (cash or in-kind). They ensure the budget is realistic and compliant.

- **Program Managers/Directors:** These are the experts on the ground. Engage them deeply to get crystal-clear clarity on specific deliverables, realistic staffing needs, and the precise outcomes the program can realistically achieve. Their input ensures the project is feasible from an operational standpoint.

- **Evaluation Staff/Data Specialists:** If you have them, bring them in early to discuss data availability, identify measurable indicators of success, and plan for robust data collection and tracking systems. A strong evaluation plan is a cornerstone of a fundable proposal.

- **External Partners/Collaborators: Never surprise your potential partners with a last-minute request for a letter of**

support. Engage them early in the planning process to confirm their commitment, clarify their roles and contributions, and secure any necessary Memoranda of Understanding (MOUs) or partnership agreements well in advance. Their early involvement strengthens your proposal's credibility and feasibility.

Sample Grant Proposal Kickoff Strategy: A Practical Blueprint

To ensure a smooth, collaborative process and maximize your team's efficiency, consider implementing a structured kickoff strategy:

1. **Distribute the RFP/Guidelines:** Immediately circulate the complete Request for Proposal (RFP) or funder guidelines to all relevant internal and external stakeholders. Ensure everyone has access to the core document.

2. **Set a Comprehensive Timeline:** Establish a realistic, detailed timeline for every stage of the grant process: initial planning, narrative drafting, budget development, internal review cycles, external partner input, final polishing, and portal upload. Work backward from the submission deadline.

3. **Assign Tasks Early and Clearly:** Clearly delineate responsibilities for each section of the proposal: who is writing the narrative? Who is developing the budget? Who is collecting attachments? Who is responsible for the final portal upload and technical submission? Assigning these early avoids last-minute scrambles.

4. **Host a Virtual or In-Person Launch Meeting:** Convene an initial meeting with the full grant team. Use this session to walk through the funder's guidelines, address initial questions, and collectively build shared ownership of the project. This fosters a sense of unity and purpose.

5. **Schedule Regular Check-ins:** Establish a rhythm of weekly or bi-weekly check-ins (virtual or in-person) for the duration of the proposal development. These meetings ensure progress, identify bottlenecks early, and allow for course correction.

Readiness Self-Assessment Tool: Your Final Check

Before you begin writing the narrative of your proposal, take a final moment for a critical self-assessment. Be brutally honest with your answers. If more than two of your answers are "no" or "uncertain," it's a strong indicator that you should delay writing and invest more time in strengthening your foundation. This pre-flight check can save you significant time and effort in the long run.

- Have we completed a thorough feasibility review of this specific program idea?
- Is the proposed project unequivocally aligned with our organizational goals and overarching mission?
- Do we have the necessary program and fiscal staff available and ready to actively support the successful implementation and reporting of this potential grant?
- Are our internal data systems and processes capable of rigorously tracking outcomes?
- Have we meticulously verified our eligibility and confirmed a strong alignment with the funder's focus?
- Do we have strong data to justify the need for this project?
- Have we engaged and confirmed all external collaborators?
- Are the proposal writing responsibilities clearly assigned?
- Is leadership available for review, signature, and approval?
- If funded, are we ready to launch on day one?

Conclusion

A great grant proposal genuinely begins long before the first word is ever written on the page. It starts with unwavering clarity, strategic alignment, and robust internal readiness. Skipping these foundational steps often leads directly to heightened stress, the submission of incomplete or misaligned proposals, and ultimately, outright rejection. But by dedicating time to build a solid foundation—one meticulously constructed on thorough feasibility analysis, strategic funder insight, strong internal team cohesion, and a keen understanding of the grant landscape—you are far more likely to submit a compelling, winning proposal that translates your vision into tangible impact.

Chapter 3: Anatomy of a Winning Proposal

Writing a grant proposal is not simply an administrative exercise—it is the act of telling a compelling, evidence-informed story. A well-written proposal makes the undeniable case for change, meticulously positions your organization as uniquely equipped to lead that change, and powerfully persuades a funder to invest their resources in your vital work. While funders vary widely in their preferred formats, specific terminology, and submission platforms, nearly all require a core set of essential components that—when skillfully woven together—form a persuasive, coherent, and utterly convincing narrative.

This chapter will meticulously walk you through the essential elements of a strong grant proposal, explaining the precise purpose of each section, how they strategically fit together as a cohesive whole, and what funders explicitly expect to see. These elements are not just arbitrary sections to fill; they are direct answers to critical questions reviewers implicitly or explicitly ask as they assess your proposal:

- **What problem are you solving?** (Answered by the Statement of Need)
- **Who is affected by this problem?** (Answered by the Statement of Need)
- **How do you plan to solve it?** (Answered by the Program Description and Methods)
- **What will change as a result?** (Answered by Goals, Objectives, Outcomes, and Impacts)
- **Why is your organization the right one to lead this work?** (Answered by Organizational Capacity)
- **How will you measure and sustain your impact?** (Answered by the Evaluation Plan and Sustainability Plan)

Executive Summary vs. Abstract: Your First Impression and the Factual Snapshot

The **Executive Summary** and the **Abstract** are frequently confused or mistakenly used interchangeably, but they serve two distinct yet equally vital purposes in a grant proposal. Understanding this differentiation is crucial for making a strong first impression and ensuring your proposal is accurately processed.

Abstract

The **Abstract** functions as a concise, factual snapshot of your project, primarily for quick reference, indexing, and internal funder database cataloging.

- **Purpose:** To offer a brief, factual summary of the entire project, allowing a reviewer to grasp the core essence of your proposal in moments. It's often used by funders to categorize proposals or determine initial eligibility.

- **Tone:** Objective, neutral, and purely descriptive. It avoids persuasive language, focusing solely on the "what."

- **Length:** Typically a single paragraph, rarely exceeding 250–300 words, unless explicitly specified otherwise by the funder.

- **Placement:** Usually appears immediately after the title page or on a dedicated abstract page.

An abstract concisely highlights the core components of your proposal—your overarching goals, primary methods, and expected tangible outcomes—without delving into persuasive arguments or detailed explanations. It serves as an informative, quick-read summary for reviewers or funder databases, allowing them to quickly ascertain if your project broadly aligns with their interests.

Executive Summary

In contrast, the **Executive Summary** is your premier opportunity to make a powerful, persuasive case for your entire proposal, designed to capture attention and compel the reader to delve deeper into your full narrative.

- **Purpose:** To serve as a comprehensive, compelling, and persuasive overview of the entire proposal. Its primary goal is to hook the reader, articulate your project's significance, and convince them of its fundability.

- **Tone:** Engaging, results-focused, and highly persuasive. It distills the essence of your argument.

- **Length:** Typically one to two pages, depending on funder instructions, providing enough space to cover all essential points compellingly.

- **Placement:** Often appears at the very beginning of the proposal, sometimes even before the Abstract, to immediately orient the reader.

Think of the abstract as a "fact sheet" for quick classification, and the executive summary as your most vital "sales pitch" or "elevator speech" for your entire project. While it appears at the beginning, it should ideally be written *last*, after all other sections are complete, ensuring it accurately reflects and effectively summarizes your final, polished proposal.

A compelling Executive Summary should succinctly include:

- The **nature and precise amount of your funding request**, clearly stating what you need.

- A clear, concise statement of the **problem or critical need** your project addresses.

- A concise yet impactful description of the **proposed solution or methodology**, outlining what you will do.

- A summary of your major **goals, objectives, expected outcomes, and anticipated long-term impacts**.

- A brief but strong statement about your **organization's unique credibility and readiness** to undertake this work.

- A clear, implied (or explicit, if appropriate) **call to action**, inviting the funder to invest.

Statement of Need: The Data-Driven Core of Your Proposal

The **Statement of Need** is, arguably, the most critical and foundational part of any grant proposal. It is where you move beyond assumption and convince the funder, with compelling evidence, that the problem you propose to address is undeniably real, profoundly urgent, and meaningfully solvable—and that your organization possesses a deep, nuanced understanding of its intricacies. If the funder isn't convinced there's a significant, well-defined problem, then even the most brilliant solution will likely be disregarded.

A strong, evidence-based Statement of Need must meticulously answer several crucial questions for the reviewer:

- **WHO** is primarily affected by this problem, specifying demographics, geographic areas, or specific populations?
- **WHAT** are the key contributing factors or underlying causes of this problem, moving beyond surface-level symptoms?
- **HOW** can this problem be meaningfully addressed, and what credible evidence (data, research) supports your approach?
- **Why your organization?** What have you already done, and what unique qualifications or insights do you possess to take this vital work further?

Key Components of a Robust Statement of Need

1. **Problem Definition: Beyond Surface-Level Symptoms** Begin by clearly identifying and defining the specific issue your project aims to address. Avoid vague generalizations. Go beyond surface-level descriptions to articulate the precise nature and scope of the problem. For instance, instead of merely stating "high dropout rates," drill down: provide current statistics, disaggregated if possible (e.g., by school, age group, or demographic), and

meticulously explain the systemic or local factors that contribute to this dropout issue in your specific community or target population. What are the consequences of this problem for the individuals and the community?

2. **Data and Evidence: The Quantitative and Qualitative Story** This is where your Statement of Need gains its undeniable strength and credibility. You must **back up your claims with recent, reliable, and relevant data.** Combine compelling **quantitative evidence** (statistics, percentages, numbers, trends) with powerful **qualitative evidence** (client stories, testimonials, expert opinions, community narratives). The data provides the scope and urgency; the qualitative stories provide the human impact.

    o **Finding Reputable Data Sources:**

    - **U.S. Census Bureau:** An invaluable resource for demographic data (population, age, race/ethnicity, income levels, poverty rates, housing statistics, educational attainment), often disaggregated down to specific geographies (zip codes, census tracts, cities, counties).

    - **Local and State Government Data:** Access data from your state and local health departments (e.g., disease prevalence, birth rates, mortality data, health disparities), departments of education (school performance, truancy rates, graduation rates), law enforcement/justice departments (crime rates, recidivism, re-entry program data), and economic development agencies (unemployment rates, industry trends, workforce shortages). Many jurisdictions maintain public data portals.

    - **National Data Portals:** Explore specialized national datasets such as CDC WONDER (Centers for Disease Control and Prevention for health data), SAMHSA (Substance Abuse and Mental Health Services Administration for behavioral health data), HRSA (Health Resources and Service Administration for health workforce and service delivery data), or the Bureau of Labor Statistics for employment and economic trends.

- **Community Needs Assessments:** Many local United Way chapters, hospitals (as part of their Community Health Needs Assessments - CHNAs), or community foundations regularly conduct and publish comprehensive needs assessments. These can provide a rich, localized understanding of problems.

- **Academic Research & Peer-Reviewed Studies:** Citing relevant scholarly articles or research findings can validate your understanding of the problem and the effectiveness of certain interventions, grounding your approach in evidence-based practice.

- **Internal Organizational Data:** Don't overlook your own data! Client intake forms, service utilization statistics, pre/post surveys, and past program evaluations can provide compelling, direct evidence of the need within your service population.

- **Surveys & Focus Groups:** Where published data is insufficient, conducting structured surveys or focus groups with your target population, community leaders, or service providers can gather powerful qualitative evidence directly from those affected.

- **Integrating Data Effectively:**
    - Instead of: *"Many students struggle with literacy in our district."*
    - Say: *"According to the 2023 District Literacy Report, **62% of third-grade students in Title I schools within our district read below grade level, a stark contrast to the 38% district-wide average.** This disparity represents approximately 1,500 students who are entering higher grades without foundational reading skills, severely impacting their academic trajectory and future economic opportunities."*
    - **Contextualize:** Always explain what the data *means*. Don't just list numbers; tell the story behind them.
    - **Disaggregate:** Break down data by demographics (age, race, income) to highlight disparities and inequities, which is particularly relevant for equity-focused funders.

3. **Root Causes and Contributing Factors: Beyond the Symptoms** Move beyond merely describing the problem to explaining its underlying, systemic, or situational causes. Why does this problem persist? This might include factors such as chronic underfunding of public services, pervasive housing instability leading to student mobility, acute workforce shortages in critical sectors, deep-seated language barriers impacting service access, or systemic discrimination. Identifying root causes demonstrates a sophisticated understanding of the issue and positions your project as a long-term solution, not just a temporary fix.

4. **Urgency and Relevance: The "Why Now?"** Make a compelling case for immediate action. Why is this issue critical right now? What are the escalating consequences if this problem goes unaddressed? Connect the urgency of your need to current events, policy windows, or emerging crises. Crucially, explicitly align your

identified need with the specific funder's stated priorities and mission, showing them *their* interest directly overlaps with *your* urgent need.

5. **Organizational Credibility in Addressing the Need:** Briefly explain what your organization has already done in this specific problem area, highlighting past successes, relevant experience, and deep community trust. This demonstrates your expertise and unique qualification to take this work further, establishing your organization as a credible and knowledgeable leader in tackling the identified need.

6. **Human Impact: Weaving the Story** While data provides the scope, a brief, anonymized story or vignette helps the data resonate on a human level. Funders are human beings, and a compelling narrative can evoke empathy and commitment. Weave in a brief story that illustrates the real-life consequences of the problem on an individual or a family, immediately connecting the abstract statistics to tangible human suffering or aspiration. Ensure these stories are authentic and ethical, protecting individual privacy.

Goals, Objectives, Outcomes, and Impacts (GOII): Mapping Your Journey to Change

Funders want to know precisely where your project is going, how you meticulously plan to get there, and how you will definitively measure success along the way. Clearly articulating your Goals, Objectives, Outcomes, and Impacts (GOII) provides this essential roadmap, moving from broad aspirations to measurable results.

- **Goals:** These are broad, aspirational statements that describe your desired long-term change. They represent the ultimate vision and are often not fully achievable within the grant period, but your project contributes significantly to them.
    - *Example:* "Improve mental health outcomes and overall well-being for underserved teens in East Oakland."

- **Objectives:** These are the **specific, measurable, achievable, relevant, and time-bound (SMART)** steps that lead directly toward your broader goal. Objectives are the backbone of your project plan and directly inform your evaluation strategy.
    - *Example:* "Reduce depressive symptoms among 75% of program participants by 20% (as measured by pre/post PHQ-9 scores) within 12 months of program enrollment."
    - *Key Points for SMART Objectives:*
        - **Specific:** Clearly defined, avoiding vague language.
        - **Measurable:** Quantifiable or observable indicators of success.
        - **Achievable:** Realistic given resources, time, and context.
        - **Relevant:** Directly contributes to the overall goal and addresses the identified need.
        - **Time-bound:** A clear deadline or timeframe for achievement.
- **Outcomes:** These are the immediate and intermediate changes or benefits that result directly from your program activities. They describe what participants will know, feel, or be able to do differently.
    - *Example:* "Participants will demonstrate increased knowledge of coping skills (immediate outcome) and report decreased school absenteeism (intermediate outcome) due to improved mental health."
- **Impacts:** This refers to the long-term, broader change that your work contributes to, often extending beyond the specific grant period and sometimes influencing systemic shifts. Impacts are the ultimate reason your project exists.

- *Example:* "Improved graduation rates within the participating high schools and a measurable reduction in juvenile justice involvement among program-eligible youth over a 5-year horizon in East Oakland."

Understanding the GOII Chain: Activities (what you do) lead to Outputs (what you produce, e.g., number of workshops) which lead to Outcomes (short- to mid-term changes) which contribute to long-term Impacts. This logical progression is often best visualized through a **Logic Model**, a powerful planning tool that we'll explore in more detail in **Chapter 4: Budget Development and Logic Models**.

Program Description and Methods: The "How" You'll Make a Difference

This section is your blueprint; it meticulously explains *what* you are going to do, *how* you will do it, and *why* your chosen methods are the most effective. It must flow logically and directly from your Statement of Need and your precisely defined Objectives. This is where you bring your project to life for the reviewer.

Key Components:

- **Overview of the Approach:** Begin with a brief, compelling paragraph summarizing your overall program model or intervention. Is it an evidence-based practice? A new, innovative approach? A collaborative model? Clearly articulate the core strategy.

- **Activities and Services:** Describe in detail the specific activities, services, and interventions that will be delivered. Be concrete:
  - What will happen? (e.g., "conduct weekly group therapy sessions")
  - How often? (e.g., "for 12 weeks")
  - By whom? (e.g., "by licensed clinical social workers")

- To whom? (e.g., "for up to 15 adolescents per cohort")
- Where will it take place? Ensure your activities are directly linked to achieving your objectives.

- **Implementation Plan and Timelines:** Provide a realistic schedule or work plan for your project. This can be described narratively within the text, or referenced as a more detailed visual attachment (e.g., a Gantt chart, see Appendix X for examples). A strong timeline demonstrates meticulous planning and operational readiness.

- **Roles and Responsibilities:** Clearly define who within your organization (and among partners) will lead each component, who will support it, and how coordination and communication will occur across the team. Highlight the qualifications and expertise of key personnel.

- **Partnerships and Collaboration:** Identify all external collaborators, community partners, and stakeholders critical to your project's success. Detail their specific roles, contributions (financial, in-kind, expertise), and how their involvement strengthens your program. Attach formal Memoranda of Understanding (MOUs) or letters of commitment as required.

This section is the operational heart of your proposal. Be concrete, use strong action verbs, and ensure every activity clearly aligns with and contributes to your stated objectives. Reviewers want to see a well-thought-out plan, not just good intentions.

Evaluation Plan: Proving Your Impact (Overview)

This section describes your commitment to accountability and continuous improvement by outlining precisely how you will track progress, measure success, and learn from your efforts over time. Funders are increasingly sophisticated, demanding robust evaluation plans that clearly demonstrate value and impact (Rossi, Lipsey, & Freeman, 2004).

Key Elements of an Evaluation Plan:

- **Evaluation Questions:** What specific questions will your evaluation seek to answer? (e.g., "Did the program achieve its objective of reducing depressive symptoms by 20%?"). These should directly relate to your objectives.

- **Indicators:** What specific, measurable pieces of data will you collect to answer your evaluation questions? These can be **quantitative** (e.g., test scores, attendance rates, number of services delivered) or **qualitative** (e.g., satisfaction survey results, focus group themes, interview excerpts).

- **Methods:** How will you collect and analyze the data for your indicators? This might include pre/post surveys, existing administrative data review, interviews, focus groups, or standardized assessments.

- **Frequency:** How often will evaluation activities occur (e.g., monthly data collection, quarterly progress reports, annual summative evaluation)?

- **Roles and Responsibilities:** Who within your organization, or what external evaluator, is responsible for leading data collection, analysis, and reporting?

You should consider both **Formative Evaluation** (ongoing assessment during implementation to inform program adjustments) and **Summative Evaluation** (assessment at the end of the program to determine overall effectiveness and impact). Funders want to see that your evaluation plan is realistic, proportionate to the grant size, and actionable—not just an academic exercise. A more comprehensive exploration of evaluation types, methodologies, and data analysis will be provided in Chapter 5: Evaluation: Demonstrating Impact and Measuring Success.

Budget and Budget Narrative: The Financial Story (Overview)

Your budget is more than just a table of numbers; it's the financial story of your proposal, explicitly detailing the resources required to implement your project. Every single line item in your budget must be clearly linked to a specific program activity described in your narrative, demonstrating fiscal responsibility and strategic planning.

Key Budget Categories:

- **Personnel:** Salaries and wages for staff directly involved in the project.
- **Fringe Benefits:** Costs associated with employee benefits (e.g., health insurance, retirement contributions, FICA, worker's compensation).
- **Equipment and Supplies:** Tangible goods needed to operate the program (e.g., computers, educational materials, office supplies).
- **Travel:** Costs related to necessary travel for project staff, participants, or training.
- **Contractual/Consultant Costs:** Fees for external experts or organizations providing services to the project.
- **Evaluation Costs:** Funds specifically allocated for evaluating the program's effectiveness.
- **Indirect/Administrative Costs:** Expenses that are necessary for the general operation of the organization but are not directly attributable to one specific program (e.g., executive salaries, utilities, rent, general IT support). Funders often have specific rules about these.

Your **budget narrative** (sometimes referred to as a justification) is equally important. It's the written explanation that clarifies the logic and calculation behind each expense, making it easy for the reviewer to understand and justify the requested amount.

- *Example for Budget Narrative:* "$37,500 is requested to support a part-time Case Manager at 0.5 FTE (20 hours/week) for 12 months, responsible for direct client intake, referral coordination with community partners, and ongoing client progress tracking, as detailed in the 'Program Description' section. Salary is based on an annual rate of $60,000 for a full-time equivalent, with a 25% fringe rate."

Always use a **Sources and Uses Budget** (which we will delve into in **Chapter 4: Budget Development and Logic Models**) to reflect both your total project income (including the grant request) and expenses, clearly showing any matching funds or in-kind support your organization or partners are contributing. This demonstrates leveraged resources and shared commitment.

Organizational Capacity: Demonstrating Readiness and Credibility

Funders need to know they can trust your organization to deliver on its promises. This section is your opportunity to highlight your track record, demonstrate your organizational infrastructure, showcase your staff's expertise, and confirm your positive community reputation. It's about instilling confidence that you are the right steward for their investment.

What to Include:

- **A Brief Organizational History:** Provide a concise overview of your organization's mission, founding, and evolution, highlighting key milestones or significant achievements.

- **Relevant Past Projects or Outcomes:** Detail prior successes, especially those that directly relate to the proposed project. Quantify achievements where possible (e.g., "Successfully served 500 youth annually for the past five years...").

- **Leadership and Staff Expertise:** Summarize the relevant experience and qualifications of key project leaders and staff. While full resumes will be in the appendices, briefly highlight their expertise here to demonstrate competence.

- **Board or Governance Structure:** Briefly describe your organization's governance (e.g., "Governed by a diverse 12-member Board of Directors with expertise in public health, finance, and community development"), if relevant, to demonstrate oversight and community connection.
- **Fiscal Health:** Briefly attest to your organization's sound financial management practices, stability, and capacity to manage grant funds. (More detail on this will be in Chapter 4).
- **Community Trust & Partnerships:** Reinforce your existing relationships within the community and with other organizations, demonstrating your embeddedness and collaborative capacity.

If this is your first time applying for a major grant, be honest about it. However, pivot immediately to demonstrating how meticulously you've prepared, the strength of your planning, the expertise of your staff (even if new hires), and any smaller successes that show your potential. Funders value transparency and a clear path to growth.

Sustainability Plan: Beyond the Grant Period

Funders rarely want to support programs indefinitely. They are strategic investors looking for projects that either lead to systemic change or have a viable plan for continuing their positive impact once the initial grant funding concludes. This section should clearly and specifically explain how your project will continue to be supported—or how its benefits will persist—after the grant period ends.

Strong Approaches to Sustainability:

- **Diversified Funding Streams:** Outline a strategy to secure other sources of revenue. This could include:
    - **Cost-sharing** with government appropriations, other private partners, or corporate sponsorships.
    - Developing **earned income** models (e.g., fees for services, product sales).

- Launching individual giving campaigns or securing major donor support.
- Pursuing additional grant opportunities from different funders.

- **Integration into Core Budget/Operations:** Explain how the project, if successful, will be integrated into your organization's core, ongoing operational budget and become a permanent part of your service delivery. This shows long-term commitment.

- **Policy or Systems Change:** If your project aims for broader systemic impact, describe how it will lead to policy changes, new legislation, or altered community practices that make the program's benefits self-sustaining.

- **Scaling and Replication:** Plans for growing the program or scaling to other areas, potentially through replication by other entities.

Avoid vague statements like, "We will seek other funding," or "We hope to continue this work." Instead, be as specific as possible, identifying potential future funders, specific revenue models, or clear integration strategies. A well-articulated sustainability plan signals your organization thinks long-term and values lasting impact.

Appendices and Supporting Documents: The "Proof"

Appendices provide essential supporting documentation that validates claims made in your narrative without cluttering the main proposal. Always refer to each appendix in the relevant section of your narrative (e.g., "See Appendix A for our detailed Logic Model").

Common Attachments and Their Purpose:

- **Logic Model:** Visualizes your program's theory of change, showing the links between inputs, activities, outputs, outcomes, and impacts (further discussed in Chapter 4).

- **Letters of Support or Memoranda of Understanding (MOUs):** Formalize partnerships and demonstrate community buy-in and collaboration.

- **Resumes/CVs:** Provide detailed qualifications and experience of key project personnel.

- **Organizational Chart:** Illustrates your organization's structure and the project's place within it.

- **Financial Statements:** Demonstrate fiscal health and management (e.g., audit reports, 990s).

- **IRS 501(c)(3) Determination Letter:** Proof of your nonprofit status (for foundations).

- **Evaluation Instruments:** Copies of surveys, pre/post tests, or data collection tools.

- **Needs Assessment Reports:** Provides the foundational data for your Statement of Need.

- **Program Brochures/Flyers:** Supplemental information about existing programs.

Be sure each appendix is clearly labeled, paginated (if a physical submission), and referenced appropriately in the narrative. Never include documents that are not specifically requested or referenced, as this can overwhelm reviewers.

Final Tips for Proposal Cohesion: Weaving the Winning Story

A compelling proposal is more than just well-written; it is meticulously **well-aligned, thoroughly well-supported, and expertly well-structured.** Each component plays a vital role, from your first sentence in the Executive Summary to the final line in your Budget Narrative.

- **Use Consistent Terms and Phrasing:** Ensure that key terms (e.g., your program name, specific problem definitions, target population) are used consistently throughout the entire proposal.

- **Make Objectives and Activities Match:** There must be a clear, logical thread connecting your stated objectives directly to the activities you propose to undertake.

- **Ensure Evaluation Measures What Objectives Aim to Change:** Your evaluation plan must be designed to rigorously measure the achievement of your specific objectives and outcomes.

- **Avoid Overly Technical Language (Unless Specific Funder):** Unless the Request for Proposal explicitly indicates a preference for academic rigor or technical detail (common in some federal research grants), strive for clear, accessible language.

- **Read the RFP Closely—and Mirror its Structure:** Many funders appreciate proposals that follow the exact order and headings outlined in their Request for Proposal (RFP) or Notice of Funding Opportunity (NOFO). This makes their review process easier.

- **Proofread Meticulously:** Errors in grammar, spelling, or punctuation undermine credibility. A fresh pair of eyes (or even two!) is essential.

- **Tell a Single, Cohesive Story:** Ensure that every section contributes to a unified narrative about the problem, your solution, and its anticipated impact.

Conclusion

A winning grant proposal truly begins long before the first word is ever drafted. It starts with strategic preparation, deep organizational readiness, and a profound understanding of both the problem you address and the funder you approach. With a solid foundation—built on clarity, alignment, data-driven insights, and team cohesion—you are far more likely to submit a compelling, winning proposal that translates your vision into tangible impact.

When these intricate parts of a proposal work together seamlessly, the result is not just a completed application; it's a powerful, persuasive case for a strategic investment in meaningful change. Funders *want* to say "yes" to projects that are well-conceived and clearly articulated. This chapter provides you with the framework to give them the clarity and confidence to do so.

Chapter 4: Budget Development and Logic Models

Budgeting is often perceived as one of the most challenging, yet it is arguably the most critical aspect of comprehensive grant proposal development. Far more than a mere tabulation of numbers, a well-structured and clearly justified budget serves as your program's **strategic blueprint**, explicitly demonstrating its feasibility, showcasing your organization's financial accountability, and illustrating effective resource management. It translates your bold ideas and well-defined activities into concrete financial terms, telling a compelling story of responsible stewardship and planned impact. This chapter provides comprehensive, practical guidance on budgeting essentials, emphasizing the development of a detailed **Sources and Uses Budget**, exploring various budget structures, detailing the critical role of the **budget narrative**, and demonstrating how **logic models** fundamentally inform your financial planning.

Budgeting Basics and Foundational Concepts: The Language of Resources

Understanding fundamental budgeting concepts is essential for preparing accurate, compelling, and compliant grant budgets. These concepts form the bedrock upon which your entire financial proposal is built (Grønbjerg, 1993).

- **Direct Costs:** These are expenses that are directly and exclusively linked to specific project activities. They are costs that would not be incurred if the project did not exist. For grant proposals, direct costs are the quantifiable resources needed to carry out your proposed program.
    - **Examples:**
        - **Personnel:** Salaries, wages, and associated benefits for staff members who spend a measurable portion of their time directly working on the grant-funded project. This includes project managers, case

managers, outreach workers, and evaluators. When calculating personnel costs, specify Full-Time Equivalents (FTEs) or the percentage of time dedicated to the project.

- **Fringe Benefits:** These are costs associated with employment beyond direct salary, such as health insurance premiums, retirement contributions, FICA (Social Security and Medicare taxes), unemployment insurance, and workers' compensation. Often calculated as a percentage of personnel salaries, these are crucial and often overlooked in initial planning.

- **Consultants/Contractual Services:** Fees paid to external individuals or organizations hired to perform specific tasks or provide specialized expertise for the project (e.g., a graphic designer for program materials, an external evaluator, a specialized trainer).

- **Equipment:** Tangible property that has an extended useful life (typically more than one year) and a substantial cost (defined by your organization's policy or the funder's threshold). Examples include specialized medical equipment, large computer servers, or program-specific vehicles.

- **Supplies:** Consumable items used up during the project (e.g., office supplies, educational materials, cleaning supplies, workshop consumables).

- **Travel:** Costs for project staff or participants related to project activities (e.g., mileage reimbursement, airfare, per diem for meals and lodging, conference registration fees).

- **Training & Participant Support:** Costs related to training for project staff or direct support for program participants (e.g., stipends, transportation vouchers, childcare during program activities).
- **Sub-awards/Subcontracts:** Funds passed through to another organization that will perform a substantive portion of the programmatic work. These are often treated as a single line item in the main budget but require a separate, detailed budget from the sub-recipient.

- **Indirect Costs (F&A - Facilities & Administrative Costs):** These are expenses that are necessary for the general operation of your organization but cannot be directly tied to one specific program or grant. They represent the shared costs of doing business and are vital for an organization's overall sustainability. Without recovering indirect costs, organizations often end up subsidizing grants from other unrestricted funds, leading to financial strain.
    - **Examples:** Rent and utilities for the office building, executive director's salary, accounting and human resources department costs, general IT support, organizational insurance, general administrative supplies.
    - **Types of Indirect Cost Rates:**
        - **Federally Negotiated Indirect Cost Rate (NICRA):** For organizations that receive significant federal funding, this is an official rate negotiated with a federal agency (e.g., DHHS, DoD). This rate specifies the percentage of direct costs that can be claimed as indirect.
        - **De Minimis 10% Rate:** Under the Uniform Guidance (2 CFR Part 200), many non-federal

entities that have never had a NICRA can elect to charge a de minimis rate of 10% of modified total direct costs (MTDC), which generally excludes capital expenditures, participant support costs, and the portion of each subaward exceeding $25,000.

- **Restricted Rates:** Many private foundations and some government grants impose their own indirect cost limits (e.g., 10% or 15% of direct costs, or sometimes none). Always adhere to the funder's specific guidelines. If a funder doesn't allow indirect costs, ensure you've covered these essential operational expenses elsewhere or factored them into direct costs where permissible.

- **Cost-Sharing and Matching Funds:** These represent contributions from the applicant organization or partner organizations that demonstrate their buy-in and help to expand the total resources available for the project. Funders often view these as a sign of commitment and a way to leverage their own investment.

    o **Required vs. Voluntary Match:** Some grants explicitly require a certain percentage or amount of matching funds, while others allow for voluntary contributions which can increase competitiveness.

    o **Types of Match:**

    - **Cash Match:** Direct financial contributions from the applicant or partners.
    - **In-Kind Contributions:** Non-cash resources that have a calculable value. Examples include volunteer hours (valued at professional rates), donated space (fair market rental value), donated equipment, or pro-bono services. Proper documentation (e.g.,

volunteer time sheets, letters from donors valuing services) is critical for in-kind match.

Common Budgeting Challenges and Practical Solutions

Even experienced grant writers encounter challenges in budgeting. Proactive planning can mitigate most pitfalls.

- **Challenge: Underestimating or Overlooking Necessary Expenses.** This is a pervasive issue that can jeopardize project implementation later.
    - **Solution:** Conduct detailed project planning sessions with all relevant team members (program, finance, HR, evaluation). Brainstorm every single item needed, from staff time and basic office supplies to specialized software licenses, data storage, external audit fees, and ongoing maintenance costs. Consult vendors or contractors for realistic quotes. Use comprehensive checklists.
- **Challenge: Lack of Alignment between Budget and Narrative.** The numbers don't tell the same story as the words, indicating a disjointed proposal.
    - **Solution:** Ensure that every major budget line item corresponds directly with a specific activity, objective, or goal described in the project narrative and timeline. Review the budget side-by-side with the narrative repeatedly. If you propose 20 workshops, ensure the budget clearly reflects the staff time, materials, and venue costs for 20 workshops.
- **Challenge: Insufficient Documentation or Justification.** Funders need to understand *why* you need what you're asking for.
    - **Solution:** Always include a detailed **budget narrative** or justification that outlines the rationale, calculation, and

purpose for each item. This is where you explain the "story" behind the numbers.

- **Challenge: Including Unallowable Costs.** Requesting funds for expenses that the funder explicitly prohibits.
    - **Solution:** Meticulously read the funder's guidelines and RFP. Federal grants, for instance, have detailed regulations (like OMB Uniform Guidance 2 CFR Part 200) on allowable costs (e.g., generally exclude lobbying, entertainment, fines, specific types of capital expenditures). Private funders may also have their own restrictions (e.g., no religious programming, no general operating support).

- **Challenge: Unrealistic Projections (Too High or Too Low).** Budget figures are not grounded in real-world costs or capacities.
    - **Solution:** Base all cost estimates on market rates, confirmed quotes, salary scales, and historical financial data from your organization. Avoid guessing or arbitrarily inflating/deflating numbers. Over-budgeting can signal wastefulness; under-budgeting suggests a lack of understanding or capacity.

- **Challenge: Poor Formatting or Lack of Clarity.** The budget is difficult to read, understand, or reconcile.
    - **Solution:** Adhere strictly to any funder-provided templates. Use clear labels, logical categories, and consistent formatting. Ensure calculations are transparent and accurate. A messy budget implies disorganized financial management.

Types of Grant Budgets: Adapting Your Financial Presentation

Grants may require different types of budget presentations depending on the funder's preferences, the nature of the project, or the source of funding (e.g., federal vs. private). Understanding these common formats enhances your ability to adapt and present the most persuasive financial plan.

1. **Line Item Budget:**
    - **Description:** This is the most common and straightforward budget format. It lists expenses by category (e.g., personnel, supplies, travel) with specific amounts allocated to each.
    - **Advantages:** Simplicity, clarity, and ease of tracking individual expenses. It's often preferred for smaller, less complex grants.
    - **Disadvantages:** It provides less context on "why" funds are needed unless accompanied by a robust budget narrative. It typically doesn't show revenue sources, only expenditures.
    - **Example Structure:**
        - **Personnel:**
            - Project Coordinator (1.0 FTE): $60,000
            - Community Outreach Specialist (0.5 FTE): $25,000
        - **Fringe Benefits (25% of Personnel):** $21,250
        - **Supplies:**
            - Office Supplies: $1,000
            - Workshop Materials: $2,500
        - **Travel:**
            - Local Mileage: $1,500
            - Conference Registration: $1,000

- **Total Direct Costs:** $112,250
- **Indirect Costs (15% of Direct):** $16,837.50
- **TOTAL PROJECT COST:** $129,087.50

2. **Revenue and Expense Budget:**
    - **Description:** This format includes both projected income (revenue) and projected expenditures (expenses) for a specific period (e.g., a fiscal year or the grant period). It offers a more complete financial overview, showing how a project or organization intends to fund its activities.
    - **Advantages:** Provides a holistic view, useful for demonstrating financial viability beyond a single grant, and often preferred for general operating support grants.
    - **Disadvantages:** May be too broad for funders primarily interested in specific project costs, or those who only want to see how their direct funds will be used.
    - **Example Structure:**
        - **Projected Revenue:**
            - Requested Grant Funds: $100,000
            - Organizational Cash Match: $10,000
            - In-Kind Contributions: $5,000
            - Program Income (e.g., fees for service): $2,000
            - *Total Revenue: $117,000*
        - **Projected Expenses:**
            - Personnel: $70,000
            - Supplies: $7,000

- Travel: $5,000
- Consultants: $10,000
- Indirect Costs: $10,000
- Other Direct Costs: $15,000
- *Total Expenses: $117,000*

3. **Functional Budget:**
    - **Description:** This budget organizes costs by the function or program component they support, rather than just by line item. It's particularly useful for complex projects with multiple distinct phases, departments, or programmatic streams.
    - **Advantages:** Clearly shows how much is allocated to different program activities, demonstrating strategic resource allocation. Helps funders understand the cost of specific interventions.
    - **Disadvantages:** Can be more complex to develop initially than a simple line-item budget.
    - **Example Structure:**
        - **Program Component 1: Client Outreach & Intake:**
            - Personnel (Outreach Coordinator): $20,000
            - Marketing Supplies: $1,500
            - Travel (Outreach): $500
        - **Program Component 2: Direct Service Delivery:**
            - Personnel (Case Managers): $50,000
            - Workshop Materials: $2,000

- Contracted Therapists: $10,000
- **Program Component 3: Data Management & Evaluation:**
  - Personnel (Data Analyst): $15,000
  - Software Licenses: $1,200
  - External Evaluator Fees: $8,000
- *Plus Indirect Costs and other general expenses allocated across functions.*

4. **Capital Budget:**
   - **Description:** Specifically details expenditures for major, long-term investments in infrastructure, facility improvements, or large equipment purchases. These are assets that will be used for multiple years and typically have a high cost threshold.
   - **Advantages:** Clearly delineates operational costs from investment costs. Essential for grants focused on infrastructure, land acquisition, or major equipment.
   - **Disadvantages:** Requires understanding of depreciation and asset management. Often subject to distinct funding cycles and review processes.
   - **Example:** Purchase of a new clinic building, acquisition of a specialized MRI machine, renovation of a community center, purchase of a new fleet of vans.

5. **Performance-Based Budgets (Emerging Trend):**
   - **Description:** In this model, portions of funding are disbursed or tied to the achievement of specific, pre-defined milestones or outcomes. It aligns financial support directly with measurable progress.

- **Advantages:** Drives accountability and efficiency, ensures funds are tied directly to results.

- **Disadvantages:** Can be complex to set up and monitor; requires robust data collection and evaluation capacity. May shift some financial risk to the grantee.

Sources and Uses Budgeting: The Gold Standard for Transparency and Balance

The **Sources and Uses budget format** is highly preferred by a wide range of funders, especially those who emphasize comprehensive financial transparency, the leveraging of resources, and a holistic view of a project's funding plan. This format clearly delineates *where every dollar for your project will come from* (sources) and *how every dollar will be spent*(uses), ensuring that total sources precisely equal total uses. It visually confirms that your project is fully funded and that you have a clear financial strategy. (For a practical template and sample, please refer to **Appendix C**.)

Beyond merely listing totals, a truly comprehensive Sources and Uses budget goes a critical step further: it meticulously details which specific funding source contributes to each line item of expenditure. This means that for every cost you list—whether it's personnel salaries, program supplies, or consultant fees—the budget actively shows whether those funds come from the specific grant you're requesting, your organization's cash match, in-kind contributions, or other confirmed funding. This granular allocation provides funders with an unparalleled level of transparency, allowing them to instantly see the full funding ecosystem of your project and understand the exact role their investment plays within it. It demonstrates not just what you need, but precisely how every resource is leveraged and accounted for.

Step-by-Step Guide to Creating a Sources and Uses Budget:

1. **Identify All Anticipated Sources of Revenue (The "Sources"):**
    - **Grant Request:** The specific amount you are requesting from the funder you are applying to.

- **Organizational Cash Match/Contribution:** Direct financial resources that your organization is committing to the project from its own unrestricted funds, reserves, or other funding streams.
- **In-Kind Contributions:** The quantifiable value of non-cash resources (e.g., volunteer hours, donated space, pro-bono services, donated equipment). Remember to document how these values are calculated (e.g., using independent sector volunteer rates, market rental rates).
- **Program Income:** Revenue generated directly by the program itself (e.g., client fees, sales of program materials).
- **Other Grants/Confirmed Funding:** Funds already secured from other foundations, government agencies, or corporations specifically for this project.
- **Individual Donations/Fundraising:** Money raised from individual donors or specific fundraising events earmarked for the project.
- **Corporate Sponsorships:** Funds from businesses that align with the project, often with marketing benefits for the corporation.
- **Example (Sources Section):**
    - Grant Request (from XYZ Foundation): $150,000
    - Organizational Cash Match: $25,000
    - Volunteer Hours (In-Kind): $15,000
    - Donated Office Space (In-Kind): $10,000
    - Confirmed City Grant: $50,000
    - Program Participant Fees: $5,000
    - **TOTAL SOURCES: $255,000**

2. **Detail All Anticipated Expenditures (The "Uses"):**
    - This section will mirror the line-item budget structure, breaking down all project expenses into clear categories. As discussed in the "Budgeting Basics" section, these will typically include personnel, fringe benefits, equipment, supplies, travel, contractual services, evaluation costs, and indirect costs.
    - **Crucial Linkage:** Every single expense listed here must directly correspond to an activity, objective, or need articulated in your project narrative. The "Uses" section is the financial manifestation of your program plan.
    - **For a comprehensive visual example that meticulously demonstrates how each expenditure line item is drawn from particular funding streams, please refer to Appendix C: Sources and Uses Budget Sample.**
3. **Ensure Balance and Provide Justification:**
    - The most critical rule: **Your Total Sources MUST equal your Total Uses.** This demonstrates a balanced, well-planned, and fully funded project. If they don't match, your budget is incomplete or inaccurate.
    - Every line item in the "Uses" section should be further explained in a detailed **budget narrative** (discussed next).

Budget Justification and Narrative: Telling the Financial Story with Precision

While the numeric budget provides the raw data, your **budget justification** (often called the **budget narrative**) is where you bring those numbers to life. It's the written explanation that complements the numeric table, providing the detailed rationale, calculation, and purpose behind every single expense. This narrative ensures transparency, clarifies alignment with your proposed activities, and is crucial for building funder confidence. It answers the reviewer's implicit question: "Why do you need this amount for this item?"

Why a Strong Budget Narrative is Essential:

- **Transparency:** It demonstrates how you arrived at your figures and that your request is well-reasoned.

- **Clarity:** It breaks down complex costs into understandable components.

- **Alignment:** It explicitly ties each budget item back to a specific program activity, objective, or outcome described in the narrative portion of your proposal. This is where the budget fully integrates with the program plan.

- **Credibility:** A well-justified budget signals professionalism, meticulous planning, and fiscal responsibility. It tells the funder you understand the true costs of your program.

- **Reduces Reviewer Questions:** A clear narrative anticipates and answers many questions a reviewer might have, streamlining their assessment process.

Tips for Crafting an Effective Budget Justification:

- **Break Down Personnel Costs:** For each position, specify the title, Full-Time Equivalent (FTE) or percentage of time dedicated to the project, the annual salary, the percentage of effort allocated to this grant, and a brief description of the duties directly related to the grant's activities. Then show the calculation.
    - **Example:** "*Project Coordinator:* 0.75 FTE (30 hours/week) @ $65,000 annual salary = $48,750. This individual will be responsible for day-to-day project management, coordinating partner meetings, and overseeing participant enrollment, as detailed in the 'Program Description' section."

- **Explain Fringe Benefits:** Clearly state the percentage used for fringe benefits and what it includes (e.g., "Fringe benefits are calculated at 28% of salaries and include health insurance, retirement contributions, FICA, and unemployment insurance.").
- **Provide Unit Costs for Equipment and Supplies:** Don't just list a lump sum. Itemize, provide unit costs, quantity, and explain *why* each item is necessary for specific program activities.
    - **Example:** "*Therapeutic Art Supplies:* $1,100. This includes 20 sets of watercolor paints @ $25/set, 20 sets of colored pencils @ $15/set, and various paper/canvases @ $300, necessary for the 10 art therapy workshops outlined in Section D."
- **Detail Travel Expenses:** Justify all travel by purpose, indicating who will travel, where, how often, and why it's essential. Break down costs (e.g., mileage @ IRS rate, per diem, airfare, lodging).
- **Clarify Contractual Services:** For each consultant or contractor, specify their scope of work, deliverables, and the basis for their fee (e.g., hourly rate and estimated hours, or a fixed price for a defined deliverable).
- **Justify Indirect Costs:** If you have a negotiated indirect cost rate, state it and show the calculation. If using a de minimis rate, clearly state that (e.g., "Indirect costs are requested at the de minimis 10% rate of Modified Total Direct Costs, as per 2 CFR Part 200.").
- **Other Direct Costs:** Any unique project-specific expenses (e.g., facility rental, printing, specific licenses) with clear justifications.
- **Connect to GOII:** The strongest budget narratives explicitly link line items back to your objectives and activities. For example, "Funds requested for the 'Community Health Worker' position are directly tied to Objective 1: To increase access to preventative health screenings..."

Logic Models: Visualizing Program Logic for Budget Development

As briefly introduced in Chapter 3, a **Logic Model** is a powerful visual representation of your program's theory of change. It illustrates the causal links between your program's resources, activities, and the anticipated results. For budgeting, the logic model is an indispensable planning tool because it compels you to think systematically about all the components necessary to achieve your desired outcomes. It directly informs the "Uses" section of your budget by highlighting every resource input required. (A comprehensive Logic Model Template and Sample can be found in **Appendix B** for your practical application.)

Core Components of a Logic Model and Their Budget Implications:

- **Inputs (Resources):** These are the resources you invest in the program.
    - **Budget Implication:** Directly correspond to budget line items. Inputs like **funding, staff, volunteer time, equipment, facilities**, and **materials** are precisely what you budget for.
    - *Example Inputs:* "$250,000 grant funds, 2 full-time case managers, a dedicated program space, educational curricula, and evaluation software licenses."
- **Activities (What the Program Performs):** These are the specific actions the program undertakes to achieve its objectives.
    - **Budget Implication:** Drive personnel time, consultant fees, travel, supplies, and equipment costs. Each activity requires resources.
    - *Example Activities:* "Conducting weekly support groups for participants, delivering monthly home visits, facilitating job readiness workshops, offering individual counseling sessions."

- **Outputs (Direct Products of Activities):** These are the quantifiable, direct products or services resulting from your activities.
    - **Budget Implication:** Outputs don't directly have costs, but the resources needed to *produce* them do. For instance, achieving "120 support group sessions" requires staff time, space, and materials, all of which are budgeted.
    - *Example Outputs:* "120 support group sessions facilitated, 250 home visits completed, 15 job readiness workshops delivered, 100 individuals receiving individual counseling."
- **Outcomes (Short- and Mid-Term Changes):** These are the immediate and intermediate changes you expect to see in participants' knowledge, attitudes, behaviors, or conditions as a direct result of your program.
    - **Budget Implication:** While outcomes aren't direct budget items, achieving them *requires* effective activities and resources that *are* budgeted. Furthermore, measuring outcomes necessitates an evaluation plan, which has its own budget implications (staff time for data collection, evaluation software, external evaluator fees).
    - *Example Outcomes:* "25% improvement in medication adherence among participants, increased knowledge of healthy eating habits among teens, improved job interview skills, reduced symptoms of depression."
- **Impact (Long-Term Change):** This represents the ultimate, broader, long-term improvements to which your work contributes, often extending beyond the specific grant period.
    - **Budget Implication:** Similar to outcomes, impact isn't directly budgeted, but the long-term vision reinforces the strategic importance of current activities and resource

allocation. Sustainability planning (which has budget implications) contributes to long-term impact.

- *Example Impact:* "Reduced rates of preventable chronic diseases in the community, improved economic stability for families, enhanced public safety, greater community resilience."

Using the Logic Model as a Budgeting Tool:

Creating a comprehensive logic model *before* you finalize your budget is a highly effective practice (Knowlton & Phillips, 2013). It forces you to:

1. **Identify All Necessary Inputs:** By clearly outlining every activity, you can systematically list all the personnel, supplies, equipment, and services needed to conduct those activities. This helps prevent underbudgeting or overlooking critical resources.

2. **Ensure Alignment:** It helps verify that every dollar requested (Inputs) is genuinely contributing to specific activities, outputs, and ultimately, your desired outcomes and impact. If an input doesn't connect to an activity, it may be an unnecessary budget item.

3. **Justify Costs:** The logic model provides the underlying rationale that feeds directly into your budget narrative, allowing you to clearly explain *why* each expense is essential for achieving your program's objectives.

Pitfalls to Avoid in Grant Budgeting: Common Mistakes and How to Sidestep Them

Navigating the financial aspect of grant writing requires diligence. Being aware of common pitfalls can save you significant time, frustration, and even prevent outright rejection.

1. **Underestimating or Overlooking Key Expenses:**
    - **Mistake:** Failing to budget for hidden costs like fringe benefits, evaluation fees, software licenses, staff training,

professional development, specific permit fees, or even unexpected contingencies.

- **Solution:** Involve all relevant departments (program, finance, HR, evaluation) in the budget planning process. Use checklists. Add a small contingency fund if allowed by the funder.

2. **Overbudgeting or Inflating Costs:**
   - **Mistake:** Requesting significantly more than is realistically needed, or inflating line items without clear justification.
   - **Solution:** Base all cost estimates on market rates, confirmed quotes, salary scales, and historical financial data from your organization. Avoid guessing or arbitrarily inflating/deflating numbers. Over-budgeting can signal wastefulness; under-budgeting suggests a lack of understanding or capacity.

3. **Lack of Alignment Between Budget and Narrative:**
   - **Mistake:** The numbers in the budget don't tell the same story as the words, indicating a disjointed proposal.
   - **Solution:** Continuously cross-reference. If your narrative proposes 10 workshops, ensure your budget accounts for all associated costs (staff time, materials, venue rental, outreach) for *10* workshops. Use a logic model to bridge the two.

4. **Vague or Missing Justification in the Budget Narrative:**
   - **Mistake:** Providing only numbers without explaining the calculation, purpose, or necessity of each line item.
   - **Solution:** Assume the reviewer knows nothing about your costs. For every item, explain "what it is, why it's needed, and how the cost was calculated."

5. **Including Unallowable Costs:**
    - **Mistake:** Requesting funds for expenses that the specific funder explicitly prohibits (e.g., lobbying, entertainment, debt repayment, certain capital improvements, or religious activities if the funder is secular).
    - **Solution:** Meticulously read the funder's guidelines and RFP. Federal grants, for instance, have detailed regulations (like OMB Uniform Guidance 2 CFR Part 200) on allowable costs (e.g., generally exclude lobbying, entertainment, fines, specific types of capital expenditures). Private funders may also have their own restrictions (e.g., no religious programming, no general operating support).

6. **Not Adhering to Funder's Specific Format or Template:**
    - **Mistake:** Submitting your own preferred budget format when the funder has provided a mandatory template or specific instructions for categorization.
    - **Solution:** Always use the funder's template if provided. Follow their instructions precisely, even if they seem unconventional.

7. **Ignoring or Miscalculating Indirect Costs:**
    - **Mistake:** Failing to request allowable indirect costs (leaving money on the table) or incorrectly calculating them.
    - **Solution:** Understand the funder's indirect cost policy (NICRA, de minimis, restricted rate). Consult with your finance department to ensure correct calculation and proper recovery.

8. **Lack of Cost-Sharing or Match Where Expected:**
    - **Mistake:** Not demonstrating your organization's commitment through match, especially if the funder values or requires it.
    - **Solution:** Actively seek opportunities for cash or in-kind contributions. Document all match meticulously and present it transparently in a Sources and Uses budget.

9. **Mathematical Errors:**
    - **Mistake:** Simple addition, subtraction, or percentage calculation errors.
    - **Solution:** Double-check all calculations. Have a second person (ideally from finance) meticulously review the entire budget and narrative. Use spreadsheet formulas to minimize manual errors.

10. **Budgeting for "Wish List" Items:**
    - **Mistake:** Including expenses for items or activities not directly relevant to the proposed project's goals and objectives.
    - **Solution:** Every budget item must directly contribute to the stated activities and outcomes of the project. If it's not in the narrative, it shouldn't be in the budget.

Practical Tools and Templates

To streamline your budget development process, several practical tools and templates can be invaluable. Full, comprehensive versions and detailed guidance for these are found in the Appendices of this book. Here are summarized references:

- **Sources and Uses Budget Template: (See Appendix C)** Guides you through organizing every dollar from its origin to its expenditure, ensuring balance and comprehensive financial transparency.

- **Budget Justification Checklist: (See Appendix D)** Helps you ensure every line item in your numeric budget has a corresponding, detailed, and compelling narrative explanation.
- **Logic Model Template and Sample: (See Appendix B)** Offers a visual framework to map your program's inputs, activities, outputs, and outcomes, which directly informs your budget development by identifying all necessary resources.

Conclusion

Effective budget development is not merely about crunching numbers; it is a profound act of strategic storytelling that communicates your program's structure, operational efficiency, fiscal responsibility, and ultimate alignment with funder expectations. By mastering the transparent Sources and Uses framework, understanding the nuances of various budget formats, and leveraging logic models as indispensable planning tools, you significantly strengthen both your organizational credibility and your chances of funding success. A well-crafted budget is a powerful testament to your organization's meticulous planning, responsible stewardship, and unwavering commitment to tangible, measurable impact.

Chapter 5: Evaluation – Demonstrating Impact and Measuring Success

Evaluation is far more than an afterthought or a mere compliance burden; it is a **strategic and essential component** of every strong grant proposal and, indeed, every effective program. It serves as a powerful mechanism for demonstrating accountability, guiding continuous program improvement, and generating invaluable knowledge that can shape future initiatives and even influence policy. Funders, as astute investors, increasingly expect applicants to articulate precisely how they will measure the effectiveness, efficiency, and broader impact of their proposed initiatives. This chapter provides a comprehensive framework for understanding the essential questions of program evaluation: **when it happens, why we conduct it, what specifically we evaluate, who takes on evaluation roles, and how we apply various methodological approaches.** By integrating a robust evaluation plan, you transform your proposal from a mere request for funds into a compelling commitment to measurable results and continuous learning (Rossi, Lipsey, & Freeman, 2004.

When Evaluation Happens: Timing and Purpose-Driven Approaches

Evaluations are not singular events; they occur at different strategic stages of a program's lifecycle. Each type of timing-based evaluation serves a distinct purpose, offering unique insights that are critical for different phases of program development and implementation.

1. **Developmental Evaluation (Before Conception/During Innovation):**
    - **Purpose:** This type of evaluation is conducted during the very initial stages of concept development, particularly for highly innovative, complex, or rapidly evolving programs where the path forward is uncertain. It's less about judging and more about learning and adapting alongside program designers. Developmental evaluators act as thought partners, helping to explore needs, test assumptions,

identify promising options, and refine models in dynamic or uncertain settings.

- **Application:** Ideal for pilot programs, new policy initiatives, or interventions addressing emerging crises where a rigid plan is impractical.
- **Example:** Gathering iterative community input, conducting rapid prototyping of service delivery models, and testing initial assumptions during the design of a novel health equity pilot program targeting an underserved, rapidly changing urban demographic. The feedback directly shapes the program as it's being built.

2. **Pre-Implementation Evaluation (Immediately Before Launch):**
    - **Purpose:** This assessment occurs just prior to a program's official start. Its goal is to assess readiness, confirm all necessary components are in place, and identify any potential roadblocks before resources are fully committed. It acts as a "pre-flight check."
    - **Application:** Ensures logistical and organizational preparedness.
    - **Example:** Before launching a new workforce training initiative, reviewing organizational capacity, confirming signed partner Memoranda of Understanding (MOUs), verifying that all necessary staff have been hired and trained, and ensuring budget sufficiency for the initial operational phase. It asks: "Are we truly ready to hit the ground running?"

3. **Formative Evaluation (During Implementation): Deep Dive**
    - **Purpose:** Formative evaluation is conducted *while* the program is actively being implemented. Its core function is

to provide **real-time, actionable feedback** for mid-course corrections, ongoing process improvement, and ensuring **fidelity** to the proposed program model. It answers the question: "Is the program being implemented as planned, and how can we make it better?" This is crucial for optimizing program delivery *while it's happening.*

- **Application:** Essential for ensuring program quality, efficiency, and responsiveness to emerging needs. It fosters a culture of continuous quality improvement (CQI).

- **Methods & Tools:**
    - **Process Monitoring:** Tracking activities, outputs, and service delivery (e.g., number of participants served, workshops held, referrals made, timeliness of services).
    - **Fidelity Checks:** Assessing whether the program is being delivered consistent with its design or an evidence-based model (e.g., observing training sessions, reviewing case notes to ensure protocol adherence).
    - **Participant Feedback Loops:** Regular surveys, brief interviews, or focus groups with beneficiaries to gauge satisfaction, perceived usefulness, and suggestions for improvement.
    - **Staff Debriefs:** Regular meetings with program staff to discuss challenges, successes, and operational adjustments.
    - **Rapid Cycle Improvement (RCI):** A quick, iterative process of planning, doing, studying, and acting (PDSA cycles) to test and refine program components.

- **Example:** Monitoring attendance, engagement levels, and collecting immediate participant feedback during the first few months of a job training program. If attendance is low, formative evaluation helps identify the reasons (e.g., inconvenient timing, lack of transportation) and allows for adjustments (e.g., offering evening sessions, providing transit vouchers). In a healthcare setting, it might involve tracking the uptake of a new patient education protocol and adjusting training for nurses if adherence is low.

4. **Summative Evaluation (End or After Program/Funding Period): Deep Dive**

    - **Purpose:** Summative evaluation is conducted at the **conclusion of the program** or funding period. Its primary focus is to determine whether the program achieved its stated objectives and delivered measurable impact. It answers the fundamental question: "Did the program work, and what was its overall effect?"

    - **Application:** Crucial for accountability to funders, assessing overall program effectiveness, and informing decisions about scaling, replicating, or discontinuing a program.

    - **Methods & Tools:**

        - **Outcome Measurement:** Collecting and analyzing pre/post data (e.g., changes in knowledge, behavior, health status, employment rates).

        - **Impact Assessments:** Broader studies attempting to attribute long-term changes to the program.

        - **Cost-Effectiveness/Cost-Benefit Analysis:** Comparing program costs to achieved outcomes or monetary benefits (e.g., "for every dollar invested, we saved X dollars in emergency room visits").

- **Comparison Group Studies:** Comparing outcomes of participants to a similar group that did not receive the intervention (though often challenging in real-world settings without randomization).
  - **Example:** Assessing changes in community health outcomes (e.g., reductions in childhood obesity rates) following a two-year nutrition intervention. Or, analyzing long-term employment data for participants six months after completing a workforce development program to determine job retention and wage increases.

It's important to remember that these evaluation types are not mutually exclusive; they often form a comprehensive, layered strategy across a program's entire lifespan.

Why We Evaluate: Purpose and Use – Beyond Compliance

Evaluation serves a wide range of organizational, strategic, and compliance goals, extending far beyond merely satisfying funder requirements. It is a critical investment in your program's integrity and future (Parks & Kaufman, 2011).

- **Program Improvement (Intervention-Oriented):** Evaluation provides concrete evidence on what's working well and what isn't. This direct feedback allows organizations to refine program design, improve service delivery, and enhance effectiveness, leading to better outcomes for beneficiaries.
- **Knowledge-Generating & Contribution to Field:** By rigorously documenting findings, evaluation helps discover what specific interventions are most effective in particular contexts. This knowledge contributes to the broader evidence base, allowing your

organization and others to replicate successful models and advance the field. It positions your organization as a thought leader.

- **Continuous Quality Improvement (CQI):** Evaluation fuels a culture of CQI, where data-driven insights are consistently used to make iterative improvements. It moves organizations from reactive problem-solving to proactive, data-informed strategic adjustments.

- **Accountability & Transparency:** Evaluation is paramount for demonstrating accountability—not just to funders, but also to the community you serve, your program beneficiaries, your board, and your internal team. It shows you are a responsible steward of resources and are committed to achieving promised results.

- **Decision-Making:** Evaluation findings provide indispensable data for strategic decision-making. Leaders can use this information to determine whether to scale up a successful pilot program, redesign a struggling component, advocate for policy changes, or even discontinue an ineffective initiative to reallocate resources more effectively.

- **Building Future Funding Cases:** A strong track record of evaluation demonstrates impact and provides the compelling evidence needed to secure continued or expanded funding from current and new grantmakers. It transforms vague claims into verifiable successes.

Understanding the primary purpose of your evaluation is the first step in shaping its design, selecting the appropriate tools, and effectively communicating its value in your grant proposal.

Evaluation Design Types: What You Evaluate

Beyond the timing of evaluation, different designs help answer specific types of questions about your program.

1. **Goals-Based Evaluation:**

- **Focus:** Directly assesses whether the program achieved its stated goals and SMART objectives (from Chapter 3). This is a fundamental type of evaluation required by most funders.
- **Example:** Did the mentoring program reduce chronic absenteeism by 20%? Did the public health campaign increase vaccination rates by 15% in the target community?

2. **Process-Based Evaluation (Fidelity and Quality):**
   - **Focus:** Examines *how* the program was implemented. It measures the fidelity of delivery to the proposed model, the quality of services provided, and the extent of participant engagement. It answers: "Are we doing what we said we would do, and are we doing it well?"
   - **Example:** Were case management sessions delivered as scheduled and as designed? What proportion of eligible individuals actually enrolled in the program? How satisfied were participants with the training materials and instructors?

3. **Outcomes-Based Evaluation:**
   - **Focus:** Centers on measurable short-term, intermediate, or long-term changes that result directly from your activities in your target population. It assesses shifts in knowledge, attitudes, skills, behaviors, or conditions. This is often aligned with funder-required performance indicators.
   - **Example:** Did participants report improved housing stability after six months? Did employees complete job readiness training with enhanced skills? Did community members demonstrate increased knowledge of disaster preparedness?

4. **Impact Evaluation (Attribution and Broader Change):**
   - **Focus:** Attempts to determine whether the program caused (attributed) or significantly contributed to (contributed) long-term, broader changes in the target population or system, often at a societal level. These often require more rigorous research designs.
   - **Example:** Did the early childhood intervention program lead to improved graduation rates and reduced juvenile justice involvement over a 10-year horizon? Did a policy advocacy initiative lead to measurable changes in local ordinances benefiting underserved communities?

5. **Cost-Effectiveness and Cost-Benefit Analysis:**
   - **Focus:** Evaluates the efficiency of a program.
     - **Cost-Effectiveness:** Compares the costs of a program to its outcomes, without necessarily monetizing the outcomes (e.g., "What was the cost per life saved?" or "cost per participant achieving X outcome?").
     - **Cost-Benefit:** Assigns a monetary value to both the costs and the benefits of a program to determine if the benefits outweigh the costs (e.g., "For every $1 invested, $3 in societal benefits were generated due to reduced healthcare costs or increased productivity").

6. **Theory of Change Evaluation:**
   - **Focus:** Assesses the underlying assumptions and causal pathways articulated in your program's logic model (Chapter 4). It explores whether the program's intended logic holds true in practice. It asks: "Are the assumed

connections between our activities, outputs, and outcomes actually occurring?" (New Philanthropy Capital, 2014).

7. **Utilization-Focused Evaluation:**
    - **Focus:** This approach emphasizes that an evaluation should be designed and conducted in ways that ensure its findings are genuinely used by specific, intended users to make decisions. It involves actively engaging stakeholders throughout the evaluation process.

Evaluator Roles and Responsibilities: Crafting Your Evaluation Team

The evaluator's role is dynamic and varies depending on the type of evaluation being conducted, the organizational setting, the specific funder's expectations, and the primary stakeholders' needs.

- **Judge:** This role typically involves providing summative ratings or judgments on program effectiveness, often for accountability or funding decisions. They assess whether a program met its objectives.

- **Researcher:** Conducts rigorous, often academic-style, investigations into program effects, contributing to the broader evidence base. This role emphasizes methodological rigor and generalizability of findings.

- **Consultant:** Offers expert advice and technical assistance to strengthen program design, refine evaluation questions, or build internal evaluation capacity within an organization.

- **Facilitator:** Supports internal evaluation efforts, particularly in Continuous Quality Improvement (CQI) models or formative feedback loops, by guiding staff through data collection, analysis, and interpretation processes.

- **Auditor:** Verifies compliance with grant terms, regulatory requirements, or financial standards. This role focuses on adherence to rules rather than program impact.
- **Coach/Supporter:** Partners with program staff to foster an evaluation culture, providing ongoing guidance and support in implementing data collection strategies and using data for learning.

Internal vs. External Evaluators: A Strategic Choice

Deciding whether to use internal staff or an external professional to conduct your evaluation is a critical strategic decision with implications for cost, objectivity, and credibility.

- **Internal Evaluators:**
    - **Pros:** Deep institutional knowledge, lower direct cost (as staff are already salaried), greater accessibility for ongoing program adjustments, fosters internal learning and capacity building.
    - **Cons:** Potential for perceived or actual bias (difficulty being fully objective about one's own program), limited specialized methodological expertise, may struggle with time constraints due to other duties.
- **External Evaluators:**
    - **Pros:** Bring objectivity and independence, specialized methodological expertise (e.g., advanced statistics, complex qualitative methods), enhanced credibility with funders, can provide benchmarks from other similar programs.
    - **Cons:** Higher direct costs (consulting fees), may require time to build institutional knowledge, less available for day-to-day consultation.
- **Recommendation:** For larger, more complex grants, especially those requiring rigorous summative or impact evaluations, an

external evaluator is often preferred for their perceived objectivity and specialized skills. For smaller grants or formative evaluations focused on internal learning, internal staff or a hybrid approach can be highly effective (GrantCraft, 2010).

Evaluation Methodologies and Approaches: Gathering and Interpreting Data

The choice of evaluation methodologies dictates how you collect, analyze, and interpret data to answer your evaluation questions. A robust plan often utilizes a combination of approaches.

1. **Quantitative Methods: The Power of Numbers**
   - **Focus:** Rely on measurable, numerical data to quantify findings, identify trends, and make comparisons. They are ideal for answering "how many," "how much," or "to what extent" questions.
   - **Tools:**
     - **Surveys and Questionnaires:** Standardized instruments (e.g., pre/post-tests, satisfaction surveys, knowledge assessments) with scaled responses or multiple-choice questions. Can be administered online, in person, or via mail.
     - **Usage Statistics/Administrative Data:** Analyzing existing records (e.g., number of clients served, service utilization rates, attendance logs, patient health records, academic transcripts, crime statistics, public service requests).
     - **Health Indicators:** Tracking public health metrics (e.g., disease prevalence, vaccination rates, hospital admissions).
     - **Performance Tracking:** Monitoring key performance indicators (KPIs) relevant to public

administration (e.g., processing times, response rates, citizen satisfaction scores).

- **Strengths:** Provide generalizable results (if proper sampling is used), allow for statistical analysis and comparisons, can be scalable for large populations.

- **Advanced Quantitative Designs:**

    - **Experimental Designs (Randomized Controlled Trials - RCTs):** The "gold standard" for establishing causality, allowing strong claims about whether the intervention *caused* the observed effects. Participants are randomly assigned to a treatment group (receives intervention) or a control group (does not). While ideal, often ethically or practically challenging in real-world program settings.

    - **Quasi-Experimental Designs:** Similar to experimental but without random assignment (e.g., using pre/post-test with a non-randomized comparison group, interrupted time-series designs). Strong for inferring causality but with more caveats.

2. **Qualitative Methods: The Depth of Understanding**

    - **Focus:** Aim to capture experiences, perspectives, meanings, and nuanced understandings. They are ideal for answering "why" or "how" questions, providing rich context and explanatory insight.

    - **Tools:**

        - **In-Depth Interviews:** One-on-one conversations to explore individual experiences, perceptions, and detailed stories.

        - **Focus Groups:** Facilitated discussions with a small group of participants to gather collective opinions, identify common themes, and observe group dynamics.

- **Observation:** Systematic viewing and recording of behaviors, interactions, and environmental factors in a program setting. Can be structured (using a checklist) or unstructured (field notes).

- **Open-Ended Survey Questions:** Allowing participants to provide free-text responses to capture unanticipated insights.

- **Case Studies:** Intensive, detailed investigations of a single entity (individual, program, community) over time to provide a holistic understanding.

   o **Strengths:** Provide rich, nuanced data; offer deep contextual understanding; illuminate underlying reasons and motivations; useful for exploring complex issues.

3. **Mixed Methods: The Comprehensive Picture**

   o **Focus:** Systematically combine both quantitative and qualitative methods within a single evaluation design to create a more comprehensive and robust understanding of program effectiveness and impact.

   o **Application:** Ideal for complex programs that need both statistical validation and in-depth narrative understanding.

   o **Example:** Using survey data to show a statistically significant increase in participant satisfaction (quantitative), then conducting in-depth interviews with a subset of participants to understand *why* they were more satisfied and to capture compelling personal stories (qualitative).

   o **Common Mixed-Methods Designs:**

- **Explanatory Sequential:** Quantitative data is collected and analyzed first, followed by qualitative data to help explain or interpret the quantitative findings.

- **Exploratory Sequential:** Qualitative data is collected and analyzed first to explore a phenomenon, and the findings then inform the development of quantitative tools for broader testing.

- **Convergent Parallel:** Quantitative and qualitative data are collected and analyzed independently, and then the results are merged or compared during the interpretation phase.

Key Concepts in Evaluation Design: Ensuring Rigor

- **Validity:** Are you measuring what you *intend* to measure?

    - *Internal Validity:* Is the observed change truly due to your program, or something else? (Crucial for attributing cause and effect).

    - *External Validity:* Can the findings be generalized to other populations or settings?

- **Reliability:** Would repeated measurements (using the same method) yield consistent results?

- **Triangulation:** The practice of using multiple data sources (e.g., surveys, interviews, administrative data), multiple methods (quantitative and qualitative), or multiple evaluators to verify and strengthen findings. Triangulation enhances the credibility and trustworthiness of your evaluation results.

- **Ethical Considerations in Data Collection:** Paramount in any evaluation are ethical practices. This includes:

- **Informed Consent:** Ensuring participants fully understand the purpose, risks, and benefits of their involvement before agreeing.
- **Confidentiality and Anonymity:** Protecting participant identities and ensuring their data is securely stored and reported.
- **Minimizing Harm:** Ensuring the evaluation process does not cause undue stress or negative consequences for participants.
- **Cultural Responsiveness:** Designing evaluation methods that are appropriate and respectful of diverse cultural contexts.

Indicators and Benchmarks: The Measurable Signs of Success

Indicators are specific, observable, and measurable signs that a change has occurred or that a program is on track. **Benchmarks** are the quantifiable thresholds or targets you aim to achieve for each indicator. They tell the funder exactly what success looks like.

- **Process Indicators:** Measure the quantity and quality of program activities and outputs (e.g., "Number of participants served," "Percentage of workshops delivered as planned").
- **Outcome Indicators:** Measure the actual changes in individuals, groups, or systems (e.g., "Percentage of participants demonstrating increased knowledge," "Average reduction in wait times for a public service").

Examples by Sector (Enhanced):

- **Public Administration:**
    - *Process:* Percentage decrease in average permit processing times for small businesses.

- *Outcome:* Increase in citizen satisfaction scores with municipal services by X% (as measured by annual survey).

- **Healthcare:**
  - *Process:* Number of patients referred to specialty care within 72 hours of primary diagnosis.
  - *Outcome:* Percentage increase in patient compliance with medication regimens (as measured by medical records review).
  - *Impact:* Reduction in preventable emergency room visits for chronic disease patients by X% over 24 months.

- **Nonprofit Services:**
  - *Process:* Number of youth participants completing 80% or more of program activities.
  - *Outcome:* Percentage of youth participants demonstrating improved leadership skills (as measured by pre/post rubric scores).
  - *Impact:* Percentage of program alumni enrolled in post-secondary education or stable employment 12 months after program completion.

It is crucial to align your indicators directly with your goals and objectives, and to ensure you have reliable means and systems to collect the necessary data.

Evaluation Budgets: How to Fund It Effectively

Funders understand that robust evaluation costs money. It's an investment in accountability and learning. As a general rule of thumb, funders often expect that **5–10% of a grant's total budget** be strategically allocated to evaluation activities, depending on the complexity and rigor required. This ensures the necessary resources are available to demonstrate impact.

Typical Costs Associated with Evaluation:

- **Personnel Costs:** Salary and fringe benefits for internal evaluation staff time dedicated to the project, or fees for external evaluation consultants.

- **Data Collection Tools:** Costs for purchasing standardized assessment tools, subscriptions to online survey platforms (e.g., Qualtrics, SurveyMonkey), or development of custom data collection instruments.

- **Data Management & Analysis:** Fees for specialized software (e.g., SPSS, NVivo), data entry services, data storage solutions, or statistical consultation.

- **Travel:** Expenses for evaluators conducting site visits, interviews, or attending data collection events.

- **Dissemination:** Costs for printing evaluation reports, creating infographics, developing presentations, or hosting stakeholder meetings to share findings.

Important Tip: Clearly distinguish between program implementation costs and evaluation costs in your budget justification (Chapter 4). While they are intertwined, funders often like to see the evaluation component transparently itemized. This demonstrates your commitment to rigorous assessment.

Building Your Evaluation Plan for the Proposal: A Practical Section-by-Section Guide

Presenting a clear, concise, and compelling evaluation plan within your grant proposal is just as important as the plan itself. Funders need to quickly grasp your strategy for measuring success. Here are the standard components you'll typically include:

1. **Purpose of the Evaluation:** Briefly state the primary goals of your evaluation (e.g., "To assess program effectiveness and inform

continuous quality improvement," or "To measure the long-term impact on participant well-being").

2. **Evaluation Questions:** List the specific, answerable questions your evaluation will address. These should directly align with your program's objectives and the funder's priorities.
    - *Example:* "To what extent did the financial literacy workshops increase participants' knowledge of budgeting principles?"

3. **Evaluation Methodology and Design:** Describe the overall approach you will use. Will it be primarily quantitative, qualitative, or mixed methods? Briefly explain the design (e.g., "A pre/post survey design with a comparison group," or "A qualitative case study approach utilizing in-depth interviews and document review").

4. **Key Indicators and Data Sources:** For each evaluation question or objective, specify the exact indicators you will measure. For each indicator, identify the precise data source (e.g., "Participant knowledge: measured by a 20-item pre/post-test," "Service utilization: tracked via client management system data," "Qualitative experience: gathered through focus groups").

5. **Data Collection Methods and Timeline:** Detail *how* and *when* data will be collected (e.g., "Pre-tests administered at intake; post-tests at 6-month mark. Focus groups conducted quarterly. Administrative data pulled monthly."). Provide a brief timeline for key evaluation activities.

6. **Data Analysis Plan:** Briefly describe how the collected data will be analyzed (e.g., "Quantitative data will be analyzed using descriptive statistics and t-tests. Qualitative data will undergo thematic analysis.").

7. **Roles and Responsibilities:** Clearly state who will lead and execute the evaluation activities (e.g., "Internal Program

Evaluator," "Contracted External Evaluation Firm," "Program Staff trained in data collection").

8. **Data Management and Reporting Plan:** Describe how data will be stored securely, maintained ethically, and how findings will be reported (e.g., "Quarterly progress reports to funder; annual summative report to board and key stakeholders; findings disseminated via website and conference presentations"). Crucially, explain *how* the findings will be used for program improvement and organizational learning.

Ensure your evaluation plan is realistic, proportionate to the grant size and program complexity, and clearly articulates your commitment to demonstrating tangible results.

Practical Tools and Templates

To streamline your evaluation planning and execution, several practical tools and templates can be invaluable. Full, comprehensive versions and detailed guidance for these are found in the Appendices of this book. Here are summarized references:

- **Evaluation Planning Worksheet: (See Appendix E)** A structured tool to help you define your scope, purpose, timing, questions, indicators, methods, and responsibilities for your evaluation.

- **Sample Data Collection Plan: (See Appendix F)** Provides a timeline and matrix outlining data sources, methods, frequency, and responsible parties for effective data gathering.

- **Outcomes Matrix Template: (See Appendix G)** Helps you connect your goals, objectives, specific indicators, and identified data sources in a clear, logical framework.

- **Sample Evaluation Report Outline: (See Appendix H)** Provides a template for structuring your final evaluation report, ensuring all key sections (executive summary, methodology, findings, implications, recommendations) are covered.

Conclusion

An effective evaluation plan fundamentally strengthens your grant proposal by demonstrating foresight, strategic thinking, and an unwavering commitment to learning, accountability, and demonstrable impact. By thoroughly understanding when and why to evaluate, meticulously designing meaningful evaluation strategies, budgeting appropriately for these essential activities, and diligently using clear indicators and robust tools, grant seekers can significantly enhance their credibility with funders. This proactive approach not only maximizes the long-term impact of your organization's vital work but also establishes a foundation for enduring trust and future funding success.

Chapter 6: Writing, Revising, and Polishing Your Proposal

Writing a compelling grant proposal is a skill that can be developed—regardless of your current level of comfort or experience with professional writing. Whether you are an emerging grant writer or a seasoned practitioner, the ability to communicate your ideas clearly, persuasively, and professionally is essential. This chapter offers detailed guidance and step-by-step strategies for writing, refining, and presenting your proposal in the strongest possible light.

The Purpose of Proposal Writing: Persuasion with Purpose

At its core, a grant proposal is a **persuasive document**. It is not just an application or a report—it is a story about a need, a strategy, and an anticipated outcome. Your goal is to convince a funder that:

1. **A Genuine, Well-Documented Need Exists:**
    - **How to Persuade:** This means moving beyond anecdotal observations to leveraging **verifiable, up-to-date data**, credible research findings, and authentic stakeholder input (as discussed in Chapter 3) to clearly define the problem. Your narrative must vividly help funders understand the precise scope, the human impact, and the systemic factors of the issue, articulating *why it matters now* and what the consequences of inaction are. Avoid generalized statements or emotional appeals unsupported by facts; focus instead on **measurable evidence** that speaks volumes. For example, rather than saying "homelessness is a problem," demonstrate the exact number of unsheltered individuals in a specific area, the demographics affected, and the contributing factors based on recent community assessments.

2. **Your Organization is Uniquely Equipped to Address It:**
    - **How to Persuade:** Beyond simply stating your organization's mission, you must articulate its **specific**

qualifications, relevant experience, strategic partnerships, and documented previous success in related work. Funders need to believe that you are not only *capable* but best positioned to deliver outcomes. Make the case with compelling data (e.g., past evaluation results), concrete examples of successful programs, and the credentials of your key leadership and program staff. Highlight community trust, long-standing presence, or unique methodologies.

3. **Your Proposed Solution is Evidence-Based, Achievable, and Impactful:**

    o **How to Persuade:** Describe with crystal clarity how your proposed program draws from **proven strategies, evidence-based models**, or recognized best practices in your field. If it's an innovative approach, explain the rigorous logic and pilot data supporting its potential. Detail how the solution can be implemented realistically given the time and resources available (linking back to Chapter 2's feasibility discussion). Crucially, articulate precisely what **measurable impacts** are expected, emphasizing the concrete benefits to the target population or system.

4. **The Investment Will Produce Measurable, Worthwhile Results:**

    o **How to Persuade:** Funders are strategic investors who demand assurance that their support will lead to meaningful, verifiable change. You must transparently detail **what will be evaluated**, *how* success will be rigorously measured (linking directly to your Evaluation Plan in Chapter 5), and *how* the anticipated outcomes align with broader community or systemic goals. This demonstrates accountability and foresight, assuring the funder that their resources will generate a tangible return on investment—not just financially, but socially.

Effective grant writing adeptly uses narrative techniques—such as unwavering clarity, logical flow, laser-sharp focus, and an appropriate tone—to transform raw information into compelling, fundable ideas. Strong proposals read like thoughtfully constructed arguments that gently yet firmly guide the reader logically from problem to solution, all delivered with compelling clarity and persuasive force. While storytelling (such as brief case examples or anonymized client vignettes) can be powerful tools to evoke empathy, always ensure they are robustly supported by verifiable data and evidence, preventing your proposal from relying solely on emotion.

Structuring the Proposal Logically: Your Grant Proposal's Blueprint

While most grant proposals adhere to a broadly standardized structure, it is the unwavering **clarity and coherence** *within* that structure that truly sets successful proposals apart. Think of your proposal as a carefully architected building: each room (section) has a purpose, but its overall functionality depends on how seamlessly the rooms connect and how intuitively the inhabitant (the reviewer) can navigate through it.

Typical Grant Proposal Components (and their interconnectedness):

As covered in Chapter 3, a standard grant proposal typically includes:

- **Cover Letter:** Your formal introduction, often signed by executive leadership. It provides a concise, professional overview and call to action.
- **Abstract OR Executive Summary:** These critical components serve as your immediate hook. The Abstract offers a factual summary for quick indexing, while the Executive Summary is a compelling, persuasive overview of your entire proposal, designed to immediately capture the funder's interest and provide a roadmap to the detailed content.

- **Statement of Need:** This is the bedrock. It presents the research-based, data-driven identification of the problem, establishing the profound rationale for your proposal based on documented evidence and human impact.

- **Project Description (Methods, Goals, Objectives, Outcomes, Impacts):** This section is your "how-to." It clearly articulates what you propose to do, detailing your specific activities, and defining your precise goals, SMART objectives, measurable outcomes, and anticipated long-term impacts (your GOII framework from Chapter 3).

- **Evaluation Plan:** Here, you detail your commitment to accountability, outlining how you will rigorously track progress, measure success against your GOII, and learn from your implementation (as explored in Chapter 5).

- **Budget and Budget Narrative:** Your financial blueprint. This section presents a detailed, justified financial plan (often a Sources and Uses budget, as detailed in Chapter 4) that precisely aligns with your proposed activities and demonstrates responsible resource management.

- **Sustainability or Future Funding Plan:** This section addresses the funder's long-term vision, explaining how your project will continue to be supported or how its impact will endure beyond the initial grant period.

- **Organizational Capacity:** This section showcases your organization's unique qualifications, experience, infrastructure, and expertise, convincing the funder of your ability to successfully implement the proposed project.

- **Appendices:** Supporting documents that provide evidence, detail, or context (e.g., logic models, letters of support, resumes).

Tips for Structuring Your Narrative for Maximum Impact:

- **Use Clear Headings that Mirror Funder Guidelines:** Always adopt the headings and subheadings provided in the funder's Request for Proposal (RFP) or Notice of Funding Opportunity (NOFO) whenever possible. This makes it exceptionally easy for reviewers to find the information they need and demonstrates your adherence to their instructions.

- **Open Each Section with a Strong Topic Sentence:** Just like a good paragraph, each major section of your proposal should begin with a clear, informative topic sentence that frames its purpose and provides a roadmap for the reader. This ensures logical flow and coherence.

- **Use Seamless Transitions Between Paragraphs:** Avoid abrupt shifts in thought. Employ transitional words and phrases (e.g., "Furthermore," "In addition to," "Consequently," "However," "To address this need") to guide the reader logically through your argument. Each paragraph should build upon the last.

- **Within Sections, Follow a Logical Order:** Whether it's the Statement of Need moving from global problem to local manifestation, or the Project Description moving from goals to specific activities, maintain a clear, consistent progression: generally from the big-picture context to the specific, granular details.

Tone, Style, and Language: Crafting Your Message with Intent

The language you use shapes how your proposal is received. A winning grant proposal is consistently **professional, accessible, and persuasively confident** (Renfro, 2024).

Tone:

- **Confident but Not Arrogant:** Project expertise and competence without sounding boastful. Use data and track record to demonstrate capability, not self-praise.

- *Instead of:* "Our unparalleled team will revolutionize services."
- *Say:* "Our team's combined 30 years of experience in this field, supported by a rigorous evidence-based approach, positions us to achieve significant outcomes."

- **Direct but Not Overly Casual:** Be straightforward and precise in your language, avoiding unnecessary qualifiers or colloquialisms. However, maintain a respectful and professional demeanor.
  - *Instead of:* "We wanna help kids with reading problems."
  - *Say:* "This program aims to improve literacy outcomes for elementary school students."
- **Respectful and Sincere:** Convey a genuine commitment to your mission and a respectful understanding of the funder's role and mission. Avoid overly emotional or manipulative language. Let the problem's urgency and your solution's strength speak for themselves.

Style:

- **Prefer Active Voice:** Use active voice whenever possible. It's clearer, more direct, and more dynamic, emphasizing who is doing what.
  - *Instead of:* "Twenty-five volunteers will be trained by our staff." (Passive)
  - *Say:* "Our staff will train 25 volunteers." (Active)
- **Use Plain Language:** Strive for clarity above all. Avoid jargon, acronyms (unless spelled out on first use), and overly technical terms unless your funder is known for academic rigor and explicitly uses such language in their guidelines. Write for a smart, generally informed audience, not just your internal team.

- **Be Specific:** Vague phrases like "a lot," "very important," "many people," or "some improvement" undermine credibility. Quantify whenever possible, use data, and provide precise details.
    - *Instead of:* "Our program will serve many people in the community."
    - *Say:* "Our program will serve 150 low-income families in the Elmwood neighborhood, improving access to healthy food for 500 individuals annually."

Funder Language Alignment: Speaking Their Language

- **Mirror the Funder's Lexicon:** Pay close attention to the specific language used in the funder's mission statement, strategic priorities, recent grantmaking announcements, or Request for Proposals (RFPs). If the funder consistently uses the term "community engagement," use "community engagement" instead of a synonym like "citizen participation," unless you need to differentiate. This signals that you've done your homework and understand their specific focus.

- **Adapt Your Focus:** If a funder prioritizes "systems change," ensure your narrative explicitly addresses how your project contributes to broader systemic shifts, using that terminology. This isn't about being disingenuous, but about framing your genuine work within their articulated framework.

Writing Techniques for Clarity and Impact: Crafting Compelling Prose

Beyond structure and style, specific writing techniques can significantly enhance your proposal's clarity, impact, and persuasive power.

1. **Start with a Strategic Outline:** Never dive directly into writing. Begin by sketching out each section's main points, key data points, and the core argument. This ensures logical flow and prevents "writer's block." Consider different outlining methods, like inverse

outlining (creating an outline *from* your draft to check its logical flow) for self-review.

2. **Lead with Purpose (Strong Topic Sentences):** Every paragraph should begin with a clear, informative topic sentence that frames the paragraph's central role in your argument. This helps reviewers quickly grasp your points and guides them through your reasoning.

    - *Instead of:* "We did a survey."
    - *Say:* "To quantify the extent of food insecurity in our target neighborhood, we conducted a comprehensive survey of 300 households."

3. **Use Formatting for Readability:** Break up dense text to improve readability. Utilize:

    - **Bullet points and numbered lists:** For presenting discrete pieces of information or steps.
    - **Subheadings:** To organize content within major sections and guide the reader.
    - **Whitespace:** Ensure adequate space around paragraphs and sections.
    - **Consistent Fonts and Sizes:** For a professional, easy-to-read appearance.
    - **Bold text:** Strategically use bolding for keywords, but sparingly, to draw the eye to critical information without overwhelming the reader.
    - **Tables and Charts:** For summarizing complex data or budgets concisely (even if these are attachments, referring to them or providing simplified versions can be helpful in the narrative).

4. **"Show, Don't Just Tell": Demonstrate, Don't Just Claim:** This is a golden rule in persuasive writing. Instead of simply stating your

program's effectiveness or the severity of a problem, provide concrete evidence and examples that *show* it.

- *Instead of:* "Our program is very effective."
- *Say:* "Participants in our pilot financial literacy program showed a **28% average increase in their financial knowledge test scores** over six months, demonstrating significant cognitive gains."
- *Instead of:* "The community needs our help."
- *Say:* "Data from the County Health Department indicates that **childhood asthma rates in our target zip code are 2.5 times the county average**, directly linked to dilapidated housing and air quality issues."

5. **Parallel Construction for Clarity:** When listing goals, objectives, methods, or benefits, use the same grammatical form (e.g., all infinitives, all nouns). This enhances readability, professionalism, and emphasizes the equal weight of each point.

    - *Example:*
        - To **increase** literacy rates among elementary students.
        - To **expand** access to after-school tutoring services.
        - To **improve** attendance rates in partner schools.

6. **Active Voice and Strong Verbs:** Reiterate the power of active voice for directness. Use strong, precise verbs instead of weak verbs paired with adverbs (e.g., "implement" instead of "put into place," "achieve" instead of "be able to get").

7. **Conciseness: Every Word Matters:** In proposals with strict word or page limits, brevity is key. Eliminate unnecessary words, phrases, and redundancies without sacrificing clarity or impact. Each word should earn its place.

Common Pitfalls and How to Avoid Them

Even with meticulous planning, certain pitfalls can derail a grant proposal. Being aware of these common mistakes—and proactively implementing strategies to avoid them—is crucial for maximizing your chances of success.

- **Lack of Focus or Overreach:**
    - **Mistake:** Trying to do too much, addressing too many problems, or proposing a solution that's too broad for the requested funding. This dilutes your impact.
    - **Solution:** Stay tightly aligned with your stated goals, objectives, and the funder's specific priorities. Use your **Logic Model** (Chapter 4) and **Funder Fit** assessment (Chapter 2) as a constant compass. Be realistic about what you can achieve with the resources and time available.

- **Overuse of Jargon or Internal Lingo:**
    - **Mistake:** Using technical terms, acronyms (unless spelled out on first use), or internal organizational language that an external reviewer—who may not be a subject matter expert in your niche—will not understand.
    - **Solution:** Write for a smart, generally informed audience. Have someone *outside* your field read your proposal to identify unclear language.

- **Repetition:**
    - **Mistake:** Repeating the same phrases, statistics, examples, or program descriptions across multiple sections (e.g., copying the exact Statement of Need into the Executive Summary without rephrasing).
    - **Solution:** While consistency is good, direct repetition is not. Introduce concepts once fully, and then refer back

concisely. Use varied phrasing to reinforce key messages. Think of each section building upon, not simply restating, previous information.

- **Overpromising or Exaggerating Claims:**
    - **Mistake:** Making ambitious claims without sufficient evidence, or setting unrealistic outcomes and timelines. This undermines credibility.
    - **Solution:** Stay grounded in realism (revisit Chapter 2 on feasibility). Ambitious goals are commendable, but they must be realistic and backed by your capacity and data. Be honest about challenges (as discussed in Chapter 9 on ethics).

- **Inconsistent Data:**
    - **Mistake:** Using different statistics for the same problem in different sections, or having budget numbers that don't align with program activities.
    - **Solution:** Maintain a "single source of truth" for all numbers, facts, and figures across your entire proposal (narrative, budget, evaluation). Conduct thorough cross-checks before submission.

- **Ignoring Word or Page Limits:**
    - **Mistake:** Submitting a proposal that exceeds the funder's specified word or page limits.
    - **Solution:** Adhere strictly to all limits. Funders may disqualify proposals that exceed these without review. Learn to be concise and prioritize the most important information.

- **Generic Language or "Boilerplate" Text:**
    - **Mistake:** Submitting content that sounds like it could be for any organization or any funder, lacking specific tailoring.
    - **Solution:** Every proposal must feel bespoke. Tailor every section—especially the introduction and need statement—to the specific funder's mission, priorities, and unique language (as discussed under "Funder Language Alignment").
- **Last-Minute Rushing:**
    - **Mistake:** Waiting until the eleventh hour to finalize and submit, leading to errors, missing attachments, or technical glitches.
    - **Solution:** Plan meticulously (revisit Chapter 2's kickoff strategy). Build in ample time for review cycles, technical checks, and unforeseen issues. Avoid burnout by pacing yourself.
- **Poor Proofreading and Editing:**
    - **Mistake:** Submitting proposals with typos, grammatical errors, punctuation mistakes, or awkward phrasing. These undermine your professionalism and credibility.
    - **Solution:** Implement a multi-stage revision process (detailed below). Don't rely solely on spellcheck.

The Revision Process: Your Multi-Stage Quality Assurance

Revision is not a single, quick pass; it is an iterative, multi-stage quality assurance process essential for crafting a winning proposal. Think of it as peeling back layers, each focused on a different aspect of quality.

1. **Content Review (The "What"):**
   - **Focus:** Is your message clear, compelling, and complete?
   - **Checklist:** Are all required elements of the RFP included? Are the goals and objectives clear and measurable? Is the proposed solution fully described and evidence-based? Does the proposal address all aspects of the funder's priorities? Is there enough data to justify all claims?

2. **Structure Review (The "Flow"):**
   - **Focus:** Does the proposal's argument flow logically and persuasively from beginning to end?
   - **Checklist:** Does the order of sections make sense? Are transitions between paragraphs and sections smooth and logical? Does each section build effectively on the previous one? Does the proposal follow the funder's requested outline?

3. **Language Review (The "How"):**
   - **Focus:** Is the writing clear, concise, engaging, and consistent in tone?
   - **Checklist:** Is the tone appropriate (confident, direct, respectful)? Are sentences clear, concise, and direct? Are paragraphs focused with strong topic sentences? Have you eliminated jargon, passive voice, and vague language? Is there strong use of action verbs? Is your language aligned with the funder's?

4. **Proofreading (The "Precision"):**
   - **Focus:** Catching mechanical errors (typos, punctuation, grammar, formatting). This should be a separate, meticulous step.

- **Techniques:** Read the proposal aloud, use text-to-speech software (it often catches awkward phrasing), print it out and read a hard copy, read it backward sentence by sentence, and have multiple people proofread it. Don't rely solely on spell-check.

5. **Peer or Expert Review (The "External Eye"):**

    - **Why it's crucial:** A fresh set of eyes, especially from someone outside your immediate project team, can identify blind spots, unclear passages, and missed opportunities.

    - **Who to ask:** Colleagues (even those outside the project), subject matter experts, professional grant writers, mentors, or even someone completely outside your field (to check for jargon).

    - **How to Ask:** Provide reviewers with specific questions rather than a general "Is this good?" (e.g., "Is the problem clearly articulated and compelling?", "Is our solution convincing and feasible?", "Do you believe we can deliver on our promises?"). Provide them with the funder's guidelines.

6. **Final Read-Through by Leadership/Finance:**

    - **Last Check:** Before submission, a final read-through by executive leadership (for overall alignment and sign-off) and finance (for budget accuracy and compliance) is essential.

Tools and Resources for Writing and Revision

Leverage available tools to enhance your writing and streamline your revision process:

- **Grammar and Readability Checkers:** Tools like **Grammarly** or the **Hemingway Editor** can provide real-time feedback on grammar, spelling, punctuation, sentence structure, and readability, helping you achieve a clearer, more impactful style.

- **Plain Language Resources:** Websites like **Plainlanguage.gov** offer invaluable guidelines and examples for simplifying complex information, ensuring your writing is accessible to all audiences.

- **Style Guides:** Familiarize yourself with common professional style guides (e.g., **APA Style**, **Chicago Manual of Style**) for consistent formatting and citation, especially if the funder specifies one.

- **Collaborative Writing Platforms:** Tools like **Google Docs** or **Microsoft Word with Track Changes** are indispensable for team-based proposal writing, allowing multiple contributors to work simultaneously, track revisions, and provide comments.

- **Project Management Tools:** While not direct writing tools, platforms like **Asana** or **Trello** can help manage complex proposal timelines, assign tasks, and track progress, ensuring key milestones are met and avoiding last-minute rushes.

- **Internal Style Guides/Boilerplate Libraries:** Develop an internal repository of consistently phrased organizational descriptions, common program models, and standard data points. This ensures consistency and efficiency, but always remember to adapt and tailor (not copy-paste) for each unique proposal.

Conclusion

Whether you're an experienced wordsmith or drafting your very first grant proposal, the writing process demands unwavering clarity, meticulous precision, and impeccable polish. By expertly organizing your content, employing clear and persuasive language, and diligently engaging in a rigorous multi-stage revision process, you can present a proposal that speaks powerfully to funders and genuinely brings your vision for change to life. Grant writing is not merely about making a request or filling out a form—it is a sophisticated act of building a compelling case for change, backed by evidence and driven by purpose. With consistent practice, thoughtful feedback, and the actionable strategies presented in this chapter, you can truly master the art of writing grant proposals that stand out for all the right reasons.

Chapter 7: Submission, Grant Management, and Reporting

Writing a strong grant proposal is a monumental achievement, but it's only half the journey. Once your diligently crafted proposal is submitted and, hopefully, awarded, the true work of effective grant management and transparent reporting begins. These post-award phases are crucial for demonstrating accountability, ensuring funder satisfaction, and building your organization's long-term credibility. This chapter offers practical, real-world guidance on navigating the intricate grant lifecycle *after* the writing is complete—covering essential submission logistics, meticulous post-award management strategies, clear reporting expectations, and common challenges frequently faced by public administrators, nonprofit leaders, and healthcare organizations. Master these steps, and you'll transform a successful application into lasting impact.

Preparing for Submission: From Final Draft to Flawless Upload

Even the strongest, most compelling proposal can falter if submission logistics are mishandled in the final hour. In today's digital age, most funders now require electronic submissions through various platforms, such as the expansive federal portal Grants.gov, foundation-specific systems like Fluxx or Blackbaud Grantmaking, or custom portals designed by individual grantmakers. This widespread adoption of digital submission streamlines processes but also demands meticulous attention to technical detail. Regardless of the specific system, precision during this final stage is paramount.

The Critical Pre-Submission Checklist:

To ensure a smooth process and avoid last-minute crises, adopt a rigorous checklist approach:

- **Content Finalization and Cross-Verification:** Before touching the upload button, conduct one absolute final review of your proposal against the Request for Proposal (RFP) or Notice of Funding Opportunity (NOFO). Confirm that all required sections are present, every question is addressed, all word and page limits are meticulously adhered to, and all figures in your narrative align perfectly with your budget.

- **Technical Formatting Mastery:** Pay exacting attention to every formatting instruction. This goes beyond simple font and spacing; it includes specific file types (e.g., PDF/A for federal grants), image resolution, character limits in online text fields, and accessibility requirements for uploaded documents. Many automated submission portals will reject incorrectly formatted files instantly, without human review.

- **Internal Approval Workflows:** For many organizations, particularly public agencies, universities, or larger nonprofits, securing final approval from various internal stakeholders is a multi-step process. This typically involves sign-offs from program leads, the finance department, legal counsel, and ultimately, your executive director or board chair. Initiate this internal review and approval process *weeks* in advance, factoring in potential revisions and busy schedules.

- **Platform-Specific Preparations:** If you're using a federal system like Grants.gov, ensure your organization's SAM.gov registration and Unique Entity Identifier (UEI) are active and up-to-date. Confirm that the Authorized Organizational Representative (AOR) has the correct permissions. For foundation or custom portals, verify user accounts are active, test login credentials, and check for any specific browser or software compatibility requirements.

Common Submission Pitfalls and Their Prevention:

- **Uploading Draft Instead of Final Documents:** A surprisingly common and devastating error. Implement robust version control (e.g., clearly label "FINAL," include dates in filenames, restrict access to the final version) to prevent submitting an unapproved or incomplete draft.

- **Missing Required Attachments:** A proposal without all necessary appendices (e.g., letters of support, resumes, 501(c)(3) determination letter, logic model) will be deemed incomplete. Develop an attachments matrix based on the RFP and physically check off each item as it's prepared and uploaded.

- **Waiting Until the Last Hour:** Technical issues are almost guaranteed to occur when you're under pressure. Portal slowdowns, internet outages, or unexpected software glitches can derail an on-time submission. Begin the upload process at least 48 hours in advance, or even earlier for complex federal applications.

- **Incomplete or Outdated Registrations:** For federal grants, an expired SAM.gov registration or an inactive UEI will halt your submission. Proactively check and renew all necessary registrations well in advance of any application deadline.

Pro Tip: Beyond the submission checklist, consider conducting a "submission simulation" with your team if time allows, especially for high-stakes or complex grants. This involves walking through the portal's upload steps with dummy documents to identify any unforeseen technical issues or workflow bottlenecks.

Post-Award Grant Management: What Happens After You Win

Receiving a grant award is a momentous occasion, signifying the funder's trust and commitment to your vision. However, this moment marks a beginning, not an end. Effective post-award management is crucial for successfully implementing your project, demonstrating responsible stewardship, and cultivating long-term, positive relationships with your funder. Your organization's internal infrastructure must be meticulously prepared to manage funds responsibly, transparently, and compliantly.

Key Elements of Meticulous Grant Management:

- **Thorough Grant Agreement Review:** This is your operational and legal blueprint. Go beyond a cursory read; meticulously dissect the grant agreement or contract with your program lead, finance department, and legal counsel (if applicable). Pay close attention to:

- **Precise Deliverables and Performance Measures:** What specific outcomes, outputs, and activities are you contractually obligated to achieve?

- **Payment Schedule and Invoicing Procedures:** Is it an upfront payment, or reimbursement-based? What documentation is required for invoices?

- **Allowable Costs:** Reconfirm what expenses are permissible under the grant. (Revisit Chapter 4 for a detailed discussion on allowable vs. unallowable costs).

- **Reporting Requirements:** What type of reports (narrative, financial, evaluation) are required, and when are they due?

- **Audit Requirements:** Are there specific audit stipulations?

- **Modification Clauses:** Understand the process for requesting budget reallocations, no-cost extensions, or scope changes.

- **Diligent Budget Execution and Fiscal Oversight:** Successfully managing grant funds means spending according to the approved budget and keeping meticulous financial records.

    - **Tracking Spending:** Establish clear internal tracking systems. This might involve setting up separate cost centers in your accounting software for each grant, implementing dedicated financial codes, and generating regular (e.g., monthly) **budget-to-actuals reports**.

    - **Allowable vs. Unallowable Costs:** Reiterate this crucial distinction from Chapter 4, providing real-world examples of common missteps during implementation.

- **Budget Reallocation and Modifications:** Most grants do not allow significant mid-project reallocation of funds between major budget categories without prior written permission from the funder. If spending patterns change or unforeseen needs arise, immediately consult your program officer and submit a formal modification request. Proactive communication about variances builds trust.
- **Cash Flow Management:** For reimbursement-based grants, ensure you have sufficient operational cash flow to cover expenses until you are reimbursed by the funder. Develop a clear process for timely submission of invoices for reimbursement.
- **Compliance with OMB Uniform Guidance (for Federal Grants):** For federal awards, adherence to 2 CFR Part 200 (Uniform Guidance) is mandatory for financial management, procurement, and audit requirements. Understanding these regulations is key to avoiding compliance issues.

- **Comprehensive Documentation and Recordkeeping:** Meticulous recordkeeping is vital not just for reporting, but for audit readiness and demonstrating accountability.
  - Maintain all receipts, invoices, payroll logs, timesheets (showing effort dedicated to the grant), progress notes, meeting minutes, and all communications with the funder.
  - Organize documents systematically, ideally in a centralized, accessible digital system, ensuring data security and privacy compliance.
- **Clear Role Clarity and Internal Communication:** Define and communicate specific responsibilities among all team members involved in the grant. This includes:

- **Program Managers:** Responsible for fidelity of implementation, achieving programmatic outcomes.
- **Fiscal Staff:** Overseeing expenditures, managing cash flow, preparing financial reports.
- **Evaluation Staff:** Leading data collection, analysis, and evaluation reporting.
- **Executive Leadership:** Maintaining high-level funder relationships, ensuring overall compliance.
- Establish a rhythm of regular internal meetings (e.g., bi-weekly operational check-ins, monthly budget reviews, quarterly strategic alignment meetings) to ensure everyone is informed, challenges are identified early, and progress is on track.

- **Proactive Communication with the Funder:**
  - Elevate this from a tip to a strategic imperative for cultivating a genuine relationship with the program officer.
  - **What to Communicate:** Proactive updates on significant successes, minor delays, unexpected challenges, major learnings, or even new opportunities arising from the project.
  - **When to Communicate:** Emphasize proactive vs. reactive. Don't wait for a problem to escalate or a report to be due. A brief phone call or email can pre-empt issues.
  - **Building Rapport:** Share stories of impact (respecting privacy), ask for their advice on related issues, and demonstrate genuine partnership.

Narrative and Financial Reporting: Telling the Story of Impact and Stewardship

Most funders require periodic reports—whether monthly, quarterly, semi-annually, or annually. These reports typically include both narrative and financial sections, serving as your primary mechanism for communicating progress, demonstrating accountability, and keeping the funder engaged. Don't view them as a chore, but as an opportunity to reinforce your value proposition and build the case for future investment.

Narrative Reports: Quantifying Progress, Sharing Insights

Your narrative reports are your opportunity to provide the qualitative and quantitative updates that bring your work to life. They should connect directly back to the promises made in your original proposal.

- **Progress Toward Goals and Objectives:** This is the core. Report on actual achievements against the specific goals and SMART objectives outlined in your proposal. Quantify your progress whenever possible (e.g., "We served 120 of our targeted 150 participants this quarter, achieving 80% of our enrollment objective").

- **Key Activities Completed:** Detail the specific program activities and services delivered during the reporting period, showing that you are actively implementing your plan.

- **Success Stories and Lessons Learned:** Integrate brief, anonymized success stories or compelling vignettes that illustrate the human impact of your work, breathing life into the numbers. These qualitative examples make your data resonate. Equally important is an honest discussion of challenges encountered, *why* they occurred, and *how* your organization is adapting or addressing them. Funders appreciate transparency and a commitment to learning.

- **Any Challenges and How They Were Addressed:** Rather than simply reporting problems, explain your problem-solving process.

Did staffing delays occur? Describe the steps taken to recruit, onboard, and mitigate impact. Did a planned activity need to be modified? Explain the rationale and the new approach. This demonstrates resilience and strategic thinking.

Financial Reports: Ensuring Fiscal Transparency

Financial reports are your quantitative proof of responsible stewardship. They should be accurate, timely, and aligned with your narrative.

- **Budget-to-Actual Summaries:** Provide clear comparisons of your actual expenditures against your approved grant budget for the reporting period and cumulatively.
- **Explanation of Variances:** For any significant variances (typically 10-15% over or under budget for a line item), provide a clear, concise explanation. This demonstrates diligent oversight and proactivity.
- **Updated Projections:** For multi-year grants, provide updated financial projections for future periods, reflecting current spending trends.
- **Documentation of In-Kind Contributions:** If applicable, transparently report the value and nature of any in-kind contributions for the reporting period, further demonstrating leveraged resources.

Pro Tip: Align reporting language with your original proposal. Use the same terms, headings, and structure where possible for objectives, activities, and outcomes. This makes it easier for funders to follow, cross-reference, and compare your progress against your initial commitments, reinforcing your organizational fidelity and consistency.

Common Reporting Mistakes:

- **Reporting Outcomes Not Tied to Original Objectives:** Presenting data that is irrelevant to what you promised to achieve in the original proposal.

- **Failing to Document In-Kind Contributions:** Underselling your organization's commitment and the total value of resources leveraged.

- **Ignoring Early Signs of Budget Over- or Underspending:** Leading to a scramble later or, worse, inability to utilize full grant funds.

- **Late Submissions:** Can lead to payment delays, damage credibility, and jeopardize future funding opportunities.

- **Generic or Vague Reports:** Lacking specific data, examples, or tailored language to the unique project.

- **Lack of Honesty:** Concealing challenges or inflating outcomes, which erodes trust if discovered.

Common Challenges and Real-World Workarounds

Even with the best planning and execution, unforeseen circumstances arise during grant implementation. Being prepared with proactive strategies and workarounds is a hallmark of strong grant management.

- **A. Staff Turnover:**
    - **Challenge:** Loss of institutional knowledge, disruption to program continuity, potential delays in service delivery.
    - **Solution:** Implement robust cross-training protocols for key positions. Document all grant activities, processes, and funder communications in a centralized, accessible location. Proactively inform your funder of significant staff changes and how you are ensuring continuity and stability in project leadership.

- **B. Delays in Program Launch or Implementation:**
    - **Challenge:** Unexpected delays in hiring, procurement, permitting, or securing partners can push back timelines and impact deliverables.

- o **Solution:** Build contingency planning into your original proposal (e.g., phased launch options, alternative strategies for achieving objectives). Most importantly, communicate any delays immediately and transparently with your program officer, requesting formal No-Cost Extensions or timeline adjustments well in advance of the original deadlines, providing a clear rationale and revised workplan.

- **C. Scope Changes:**
    - o **Challenge:** The temptation to alter the project's scope or objectives without funder approval.
    - o **Solution:** Any significant changes to the project's scope, core objectives, or key activities *must* be submitted as formal amendment requests to the funder *as early as possible*. Always secure prior written approval before implementing deviations. This maintains ethical integrity and contractual compliance.

- **D. Partner Underperformance or Changes:**
    - o **Challenge:** A collaborating partner fails to deliver on their commitments or experiences internal changes that impact their participation.
    - o **Solution:** Formalize partnerships with clear Memoranda of Understanding (MOUs) detailing roles, responsibilities, and deliverables. Schedule regular partner check-ins to monitor progress and address issues early. If an issue arises, address it directly with the partner; if it impacts the grant significantly, involve the funder in finding a solution, potentially leading to a replacement partner or revised scope.

- **E. Regulatory or Political Shifts:**
    - **Challenge:** Changes in government regulations, policy priorities, or political administrations can impact grant rules, allowable activities, or the general funding climate.
    - **Solution:** Continuously monitor relevant policy trends and subscribe to federal agency updates (for government grants). Document how the external environment impacts your program in progress reports, and be prepared to adapt your approach or seek flexibility from funders where possible.

- **F. Unexpected Budgetary Surpluses or Shortfalls:**
    - **Challenge:** Underspending may indicate poor planning or under-delivery; overspending can lead to financial strain or misuse of funds.
    - **Solution:** Conduct regular (e.g., monthly) budget-to-actual reviews with your finance department. If significant variances occur, proactively request budget modifications or permission to reallocate funds within the funder's guidelines. Never make assumptions; always seek prior approval.

Grant Closeout and Sustainability: Ensuring Lasting Impact

As a grant nears its completion, a meticulous closeout process is as crucial as the initial submission and ongoing management. This final phase involves not only wrapping up deliverables and financial records but also strategically ensuring the sustainability of outcomes and impacts where possible.

Closeout Best Practices:

- **Submit Final Reports On Time:** This includes final narrative, financial, and evaluation reports. Timely submission is a non-negotiable step for compliance and maintaining an excellent funder relationship, crucial for future opportunities.

- **Financial Reconciliation:** Ensure all expenditures are meticulously reconciled with your accounting records and match the final financial report. Resolve any discrepancies immediately.

- **Asset Disposition:** If the grant funded significant equipment or property, understand and comply with the funder's rules for asset disposition (e.g., do you keep it, donate it, or must it be returned?).

- **Final Documentation Archive:** Create a comprehensive, well-organized, and accessible archive of all grant-related records. This should include all proposals, agreements, reports, communications, financial documentation, and evaluation data. This prepares you for potential audits and serves as a vital institutional historical record.

- **Conduct Internal Debriefs:** Gather your project team and key stakeholders for a final debriefing session. Capture lessons learned, document successes and challenges, and identify recommendations for future programs and grant strategies. This institutional knowledge is invaluable for continuous improvement.

- **Host a Debrief with the Funder (if appropriate):** Offer to meet with your program officer to discuss the grant's overall outcomes, share key learnings, and express your gratitude. This professional courtesy can significantly strengthen relationships, regardless of whether you anticipate immediate future funding from them.

- **Acknowledge Funders Publicly:** Where appropriate and permissible by the funder's guidelines, ensure proper and prominent public acknowledgment of their support through annual reports, websites, or other communications.

Sustainability Planning (Strategic Continuation):

Reiterating and reinforcing concepts from Chapter 3, with a focus on active implementation post-award:

- **Identify and Cultivate Alternative Funding Sources Early:** Sustainability is not a last-minute scramble. Begin cultivating a diversified portfolio of revenue streams (e.g., individual giving, corporate sponsorships, earned income models, other grant opportunities) from the very beginning of the grant-funded program.

- **Build Internal Capacity:** Invest in strengthening your organization's internal capacity for ongoing fundraising, program delivery, and evaluation. This reduces over-reliance on any single funding stream and fosters long-term self-sufficiency.

- **Document Program Outcomes to Support Future Proposals:** Your final evaluation report and meticulously documented successes are your most powerful fundraising tools. Leverage these compelling outcomes to articulate your impact and build strong cases for continued funding or new grant applications.

- **Program Integration:** For programs that prove highly successful and align with your core mission, strategically plan for their integration into your organization's permanent, ongoing operations, ideally supported by diversified and stable revenue streams.

Pro Tip: Your final grant report, particularly the narrative outlining your achievements and the outcome data from your evaluation, serves as an invaluable foundation for future funding applications. Repurpose and refine its compelling content to showcase your successes and articulate the continued need for your vital work.

Conclusion: Managing the Full Lifecycle of a Grant

Grant success extends far beyond the moment a proposal is awarded; it encompasses a rigorous commitment to meticulous implementation, unwavering accountability, and strategic trust-building throughout the entire grant lifecycle. Public agencies, nonprofit organizations, and healthcare systems that master the art of effective grant management position themselves not just for the successful execution of one project, but for long-term organizational sustainability and significantly stronger, enduring funder relationships. By preparing thoroughly for submission, communicating proactively during the grant term, meticulously managing resources, ethically addressing challenges, and closing out effectively, you consistently demonstrate that your organization is a wise, impactful, and trustworthy investment—not just once, but again and again.

Chapter 8: Real-World Grant Proposals – An Illustrative Analysis

This chapter serves as a pivotal bridge, transforming the theoretical knowledge and strategic frameworks from earlier chapters into actionable insights. Here, we'll examine two anonymized grant proposals written by your graduate students—"Clean Hands: Brighter and Healthier Future" (**Appendix I**) and "Smart Moves: Bunche Edition" (**Appendix J**). These examples, developed in response to real or simulated funding opportunities, powerfully showcase the application of structured writing, thoughtful planning, and persuasive reasoning.

This analysis provides a section-by-section review of each proposal, highlighting how they successfully illustrate key elements discussed in previous chapters, identifying subtle opportunities for even greater enhancement, and linking lessons back to the foundational principles of effective grant writing. By studying these real-world applications, you'll gain a deeper understanding of how abstract concepts translate into compelling, fundable proposals.

Proposal Summaries

- **Clean Hands: Brighter and Healthier Future:** This proposal from First 5 Sacramento outlines a proactive, school-based hygiene education pilot program. It aims to prevent the spread of illness and improve student health and attendance among transitional kindergarten (TK) students in socioeconomically disadvantaged areas of the Sacramento City Unified School District.

- **Smart Moves: Bunche Edition:** Partnership for a Healthier America's 'Smart Moves: Bunche Edition' program introduces an equity-focused after-school program. It's designed to address childhood obesity in Compton, California, through a comprehensive strategy of nutrition education, behavior modification, and physical activity classes for middle school students and their families.

Both proposals demonstrate remarkable initiative, clarity of purpose, and practical program thinking. They offer valuable insights into crafting a grant application, while also providing useful moments for learning and refinement that can benefit any aspiring grant writer.

1. Abstract & Executive Summary: Crafting a Compelling Snapshot

These initial sections are your proposal's first impression, determining whether a funder will delve deeper.

Clean Hands: Brighter and Healthier Future: The "Clean Hands" proposal opens with a clear, straightforward abstract. It immediately outlines the public health issue of poor hand hygiene among elementary students, identifies absenteeism as a key problem, and positions the program as a preventative intervention. The tone is informative and concise, demonstrating an appropriate alignment with the goals of school-based health promotion. This abstract effectively functions as a quick fact sheet for the reviewer.

Opportunities for Enhanced Clarity: While effective in its clarity, consider how even more concrete statistics on current absenteeism or infection rates, or a brief mention of key distinguishing program components (like UV-sensitive gels or family involvement strategies), could further sharpen this immediate snapshot for quick funder review, maximizing that critical first impression (revisit **Chapter 3** for Executive Summary guidance).

Smart Moves: Bunche Edition: The "Smart Moves" proposal features a more engaging and immediate abstract that quickly establishes the urgency of childhood obesity and the context for its youth development initiative. It introduces the target population and the multifaceted problem—encompassing limited access to healthy foods, poor health education, and unsafe areas for physical activity—while connecting these issues to broader systemic disparities. The writing here is confident and polished, effectively capturing the reader's attention and setting a persuasive tone from the start.

Opportunities for Deeper Impact: To build on this strong opening, the summary could subtly enhance its conciseness and ensure every sentence is packed with maximum information. Readers benefit when they come away with a vivid snapshot of both the problem and the proposed solution within just a few compelling sentences, clearly outlining the program's core components and anticipated outcomes (reflecting the guidance in **Chapter 3**).

Lesson: Hooking the Reader from the Start Executive summaries and abstracts serve as your proposal's vital first impression. As explored in **Chapter 3**, the abstract is your factual snapshot for quick reference and indexing, while the executive summary acts as your persuasive "sales pitch." Both should be meticulously crafted to balance detail with conciseness, starting strong with a clear statement of need and proposed solution. Incorporating one or two compelling statistics or concrete facts early on can immediately establish the problem's urgency and the relevance of your approach, ensuring the funder quickly grasps your vision and its significance.

2. Statement of Need: The Data-Driven Foundation Illustrated

The Statement of Need is the bedrock of your proposal, demonstrating the problem's reality and your deep understanding of it.

Clean Hands: Brighter and Healthier Future: The "Clean Hands" proposal commendably identifies poor hand hygiene as a major contributor to student illness and absenteeism. It references general health data linking handwashing practices to disease prevention and emphasizes the cost to educational outcomes when students miss class due to preventable illness. This solid framing establishes the importance of the issue.

Opportunities for Deeper Impact: To build on this strong foundation, future proposals could explore incorporating even more localized, real-time data from the Sacramento City Unified School District on student absenteeism rates or specific infection rates within the target schools (revisiting **Chapter 3** on finding reputable local data sources). Additionally, a brief, compelling quote or anonymized anecdote from a local teacher or school nurse could personalize the data, creating an even stronger emotional and contextual connection to the targeted communities.

Smart Moves: Bunche Edition: The "Smart Moves" proposal provides a much richer and more compelling context for its case. It offers specific, well-cited data on childhood obesity prevalence, middle school academic performance metrics, and behavioral health issues within its targeted Service Planning Area (SPA-6) in Los Angeles County. The narrative cites relevant and reliable data sources, such as school district reports, public health data, and youth wellness studies. By seamlessly integrating both robust quantitative data and insightful contextual explanations (e.g., food deserts, lack of safe play spaces), this proposal successfully presents an urgent and multifaceted rationale for its intervention.

Lesson: Localized Data Strengthens Credibility As highlighted in **Chapter 3**, a compelling Statement of Need is fundamentally data-driven. Both proposals illustrate the power of grounding your claims in verifiable, localized data, whether quantitative (statistics on absenteeism, obesity rates) or qualitative (insights into contributing factors). Avoid broad generalizations; instead, meticulously tie the need directly to your target population and geographic area. By combining robust evidence with an understanding of the problem's root causes and human impact, you build an unassailable case for your project's necessity.

3. Program Design & Methodology: The "How" You'll Achieve Change

This section details your program's approach, demonstrating its feasibility and effectiveness.

Clean Hands: Brighter and Healthier Future: The "Clean Hands" proposal presents a clear, well-organized sequence of activities designed to promote hand hygiene. These include interactive student workshops, informative newsletters for parents, and the distribution of practical hygiene kits. The activities are thoughtfully designed to be appropriate for the transitional kindergarten target audience, suggesting a solid understanding of age-appropriate educational delivery. The use of tools like

UV-sensitive gels and role-playing demonstrates a creative and engaging approach to health education.

Opportunities for Enhanced Clarity: For maximizing funder confidence in implementation and long-term sustainability, future proposals could benefit from a more explicit integration of a **Logic Model** (as detailed in **Chapter 4**), or a more comprehensive explanation of how each specific activity directly supports the intended health outcomes and behavioral changes. For example, explicitly detailing the connection between distributing hygiene kits and reducing absenteeism with supporting research or theory could strengthen the methodological rigor.

Smart Moves: Bunche Edition: The "Smart Moves" proposal presents a layered and thoughtful program that combines nutrition education, behavior modification classes, and consistent physical activity sessions, complemented by family engagement strategies. It demonstrates a strong understanding of youth development theory and meticulously connects its chosen methods to the clearly identified needs of the target population. The strategic use of peer mentors, in particular, reflects a strength-based, community-engaged approach that fosters sustainability.

Opportunities for Deeper Assurance: While comprehensive, future proposals could provide slightly more granular detail about the precise roles and contributions of all partner organizations (e.g., Bunche Middle School, specific community health clinics). Further elaboration on the exact logistics of implementation (e.g., exact schedules, curriculum details) and the specific training and ongoing support provided to peer mentors could enhance funder confidence in the program's operational feasibility and quality (reflecting the depth discussed in **Chapter 3**).

Lesson: Strategic Design Meets Operational Detail Funders seek both inspiration and assurance in your program design. As illustrated by both proposals, strong applications combine innovative or evidence-based ideas with detailed operational plans. Clearly articulating *what* you will do and *how* you will do it—including specific activities, staffing, timelines, and partnerships—is essential. This demonstrates not just a compelling vision, but also the practical foresight and capacity to execute your program effectively.

4. Goals, Objectives, Outcomes, and Impacts (GOII): Defining Success with Precision

This section articulates your project's intended results, allowing funders to envision the change their investment will bring.

Clean Hands: Brighter and Healthier Future: The "Clean Hands" proposal articulates clear, relevant goals around improving hygiene awareness and reducing student illness, and includes objectives related to participation in workshops and distribution of materials. This demonstrates a foundational understanding of setting project aims.

Opportunities for Precision: To maximize clarity and create a more robust framework for evaluation, consider refining all objectives to consistently meet the **SMART** criteria (Specific, Measurable, Achievable, Relevant, Time-bound). Explicitly including time-bound targets and clear outcome percentages (e.g., "reduce illness-related absences by 10% by June 2027") would significantly strengthen this section, providing funders with a precise picture of anticipated success (revisit **Chapter 3** for detailed GOII guidance).

Smart Moves: Bunche Edition: The "Smart Moves" proposal features remarkably well-developed **SMART objectives** focused on tangible improvements such as GPA increases, reduction in behavioral referrals, and increased parental involvement. These objectives are meticulously aligned with the program activities described, and the proposal includes a clear plan for tracking these outcomes. The impact statements are particularly strong, effectively positioning the program within a broader school climate and college-readiness framework, offering funders a compelling vision of long-term change.

Lesson: Measurable Objectives Drive Accountability As emphasized in **Chapter 3**, clear, measurable objectives are paramount for demonstrating accountability and enabling effective evaluation. Both proposals illustrate the critical step of translating broad goals into specific, actionable, and measurable outcomes. Employing the SMART framework consistently for your objectives and clearly articulating the anticipated outputs, outcomes, and long-term impacts helps funders easily envision what success looks like and how their investment will generate worthwhile results. Using tables or bullet points can also significantly increase the clarity and scannability of your GOII statements.

5. Evaluation Plan: Proving Your Impact

Your evaluation plan demonstrates your commitment to learning, accountability, and continuous improvement.

Clean Hands: Brighter and Healthier Future: While the "Clean Hands" proposal commendably mentions data collection to track program reach and participant satisfaction, demonstrating an understanding of evaluation's role, it primarily outlines the *types* of evaluation. It suggests using school nurse observations, parent surveys, and attendance records, which are excellent data sources.

Opportunities for Enhanced Rigor: To further strengthen the evaluation framework, future plans might explicitly detail the specific data collection tools (e.g., naming the survey instruments, describing the observation checklist) and methodologies (e.g., pre/post design for surveys, quantitative analysis of attendance data, qualitative analysis of open-ended feedback). A clear delineation of roles for evaluation oversight (e.g., identifying the project manager, school nurse, or an external evaluator, as discussed in **Chapter 5**) would underscore the commitment to rigorous, systematic assessment.

Smart Moves: Bunche Edition: The "Smart Moves" proposal presents a more robust evaluation plan, thoughtfully incorporating both formative feedback mechanisms (such as student and parent surveys, mid-program check-ins with staff) and summative outcomes (e.g., changes in GPA, school behavior data, BMI percentile). It identifies several diverse data sources and describes how feedback will be used to adapt programming, reflecting a commitment to continuous improvement.

Opportunities for Deeper Clarity: While strong, this plan could be further enhanced by including a more detailed timeline of specific evaluation activities (e.g., when baseline data is collected, when mid-point reports are generated, when final impact analysis occurs). Explicitly specifying who will lead each aspect of the evaluation effort—whether internal staff, a contracted external evaluator, or a blend of both (refer to **Chapter 5** on evaluator roles)—would add another layer of clarity and assure funders of dedicated resources.

Lesson: Rigorous Evaluation Builds Confidence As explored in **Chapter 5**, a robust evaluation plan is not merely about reporting; it's about genuine learning, accountability, and demonstrating impact. Both proposals illustrate the essential step of defining how success will be measured. Stronger proposals clearly define evaluation questions, methodologies, indicators, and roles. This meticulous planning communicates confidence in your program's ability to achieve results and your commitment to transparently sharing its impact.

6. Budget & Justification: The Financial Story

Your budget is the financial blueprint of your program, demonstrating fiscal responsibility and alignment.

Clean Hands: Brighter and Healthier Future: The "Clean Hands" proposal includes a clear line-item budget that outlines categories such as personnel, materials, and instructional costs. While the amounts seem reasonable and the budget does not appear excessive, the accompanying budget narrative provides a good start, explaining general categories.

Opportunities for Deeper Transparency: To fully harness the power of the budget as a storytelling tool (as discussed in **Chapter 4**), future iterations could provide a more granular narrative explaining *why* each line item is necessary and *how* costs were precisely estimated. For example, breaking down "Program Materials" to list specific items like "UV-sensitive gels" or "handwashing kits" with unit costs would add clarity. Explicitly showcasing any **in-kind contributions** or **matching funds** (e.g., volunteer hours, donated school space) would further demonstrate leveraged resources and the community's investment in the program.

Smart Moves: Bunche Edition: The "Smart Moves" proposal provides a more detailed budget that reflects its multifaceted programming, including specific categories for staff time, transportation, meals for youth, and evaluation tools. The accompanying budget narrative diligently justifies each cost, demonstrating an understanding of tying expenses to program activities.

Opportunities for Strategic Linkage: While strong, the justification could go further by explicitly connecting each expense to specific program outcomes. For instance, the rationale behind staff FTEs, mentoring stipends, or specific equipment purchases could be tied directly to particular objectives for youth engagement or academic success. This approach elevates the budget from a list of costs to a direct investment in measurable change, reinforcing concepts from **Chapter 4** on budget alignment and justification.

Lesson: Budgets Tell a Strategic Story As emphasized in **Chapter 4**, a proposal's budget should tell a cohesive financial story that precisely aligns with the program narrative. Both proposals illustrate the effort to allocate resources. However, truly compelling budgets feature a detailed narrative that justifies every line item, explains its calculation, and explicitly ties each expense to specific program activities, objectives, and anticipated outcomes. Demonstrating cost-effectiveness, transparency, and the leveraging of all resources (including in-kind contributions) significantly enhances funder confidence.

7. Writing Style & Formatting: The Professional Polish

The way your proposal looks and reads is as important as its content; it's a direct reflection of your organization's professionalism.

Clean Hands: Brighter and Healthier Future: The "Clean Hands" proposal is generally well-organized, with a logical structure and appropriate use of headings. The writing is easy to follow and conveys the program's purpose clearly. This demonstrates a solid grasp of fundamental proposal presentation.

Opportunities for Enhanced Polish: While clear, exploring techniques for varying sentence structure and ensuring even tighter transitions between sections can further sharpen its professional tone (as explored in **Chapter 6**). A meticulous final review for any minor formatting inconsistencies (e.g., slight variations in font sizes or spacing) can also elevate the overall professional presentation.

Smart Moves: Bunche Edition: The "Smart Moves" proposal showcases a confident, persuasive, and engaging writing style. The narrative flows smoothly, and the judicious formatting choices (clear headings, effective use of bullet points and whitespace) make it easy to scan and digest key information. The overall tone is assertive and professional, reflecting the organization's mission.

Opportunities for Refinement: Minor instances of wordiness or overly long paragraphs can occasionally interrupt the rhythm of an otherwise strong narrative. A final, rigorous grammar, punctuation, and spell check would resolve any small inconsistencies, pushing this proposal to an even higher level of professional polish (reiterating the importance of the revision process in **Chapter 6**).

Lesson: Professionalism in Every Detail As detailed in **Chapter 6**, meticulous editing for tone, clarity, and flow is paramount. Both proposals effectively demonstrate that strong ideas are best conveyed through a professional and polished presentation. Consistent use of headings, precise grammar, and concise language are not mere formalities. They are fundamental elements that elevate your proposal's credibility and ensure your message is received with the seriousness and attention it deserves.

8. Overarching Lessons Learned & Best Practices from Real-World Proposals

Analyzing these student proposals reveals universal truths about successful grant writing that apply across all sectors and funding opportunities.

- **Clarity Drives Persuasion:** Both "Clean Hands" and "Smart Moves" demonstrate that the fundamental clarity of your mission, the problem you address, and your proposed strategy is the bedrock of persuasion. When reviewers can easily understand *what* you propose and *why* it matters, your chances of success increase dramatically. A clear, well-articulated vision, translated into precise goals and objectives, makes it easy for funders to say "yes."

- **Data-Driven Foundations Build Unassailable Credibility:** As highlighted in both proposals' Statements of Need, the strategic integration of robust, localized data (both quantitative statistics and compelling qualitative narratives) is absolutely critical. This evidence from reputable sources moves your proposal beyond good intentions to demonstrate a deep, verifiable understanding of the problem and its urgency. Data grounds your story in reality.

- **Details Transform Ideas into Feasibility:** While a compelling idea is essential, these proposals underscore that meticulous operational detail wins grants. Funders need assurance that you've thought through the "who, what, when, where, why, and how." A clear program design, detailed activities, a logical timeline, and identified roles—all components that directly inform your budget and evaluation plans—demonstrate your organization's capacity and foresight, building immense confidence in your ability to execute.

- **Evaluation Fuels Confidence and Continuous Learning:** Both proposals highlight the recognition that a thoughtful plan for data collection, analysis, and utilization is vital. A robust evaluation framework not only increases funder confidence in your ability to measure impact but also fuels continuous program improvement. It demonstrates that your organization is committed to accountability and learning, turning results into stronger future programs.

- **Professional Presentation Reflects Organizational Professionalism:** The overall writing style, tone, and meticulous formatting are not superficial elements; they are direct reflections of your organization's competence, attention to detail, and respect for the funder's time. A polished proposal signals an organized, capable organization that is serious about its work and committed to excellence in all its endeavors.

- **The Power of Interconnectedness:** These analyses reveal that a winning proposal is not a collection of isolated sections but a deeply interconnected narrative. Every component—from the Statement of Need to the Budget, from the Program Design to the Evaluation Plan—must reinforce the others, telling a single, cohesive, and compelling story. A weakness in one area (e.g., a vague objective) can subtly undermine the credibility of otherwise strong sections.

- **Strategic Alignment is Paramount:** The comparison of these proposals, particularly in their approach to funder alignment, emphasizes the critical thinking involved in tailoring your project to a specific funder's mission and priorities. It's about demonstrating *why your unique work is the perfect fit* for *their specific funding goals*.

- **Iterative Improvement is the Pathway to Mastery:** Finally, examining these strong student examples provides a crucial meta-lesson: grant writing is an iterative process. It involves continuous learning, refinement, and adaptation. By analyzing strengths and areas for growth, much like these proposals illustrate, you can continuously hone your skills and transform your approach into a consistent pathway to funding success.

Readers are encouraged to review the full proposals in **Appendix I: Sample Grant Proposal 1 ('Clean Hands: Brighter and Healthier Future')** and **Appendix J: Sample Grant Proposal 2 ('Smart Moves: Bunche Edition')**, mark up each section with this book's guidance in mind, and consider how they'd improve or adapt them for their own efforts.

Conclusion: From Student Work to Field Readiness

This chapter brings the full journey of the grant writing process into sharp focus. By systematically studying real-world examples, you, as future grant writers, can gain invaluable insights into how core concepts translate into practice—and where opportunities for optimization often arise. Grant writing, as demonstrated by these thoughtful proposals, is a complex, iterative, and profoundly strategic skill. But it is, fundamentally, learnable. With unwavering clarity of purpose, meticulous attention to structure and detail, and an enduring commitment to rigorous revision and ethical practice, your next proposal can not only meet expectations but consistently exceed them, effectively turning your vision into a tangible, impactful reality for your community.

Chapter 9: Beyond the Application — Ethics, Integrity, and Responsibility in Grant Writing

Many years ago, while serving as an executive at Volunteers of America in the San Francisco Bay Area, I successfully secured significant funding from the California Department of Corrections to support vital transitional case management and community-based rehabilitation programs. That success, a testament to the program's impact, naturally led to multiple requests for consulting support from other earnest nonprofits seeking similar funding opportunities in different parts of the state.

One such organization enthusiastically hired me to guide them through their proposal development process. I provided comprehensive technical assistance, shared key strategic insights, and even walked them through a detailed sample proposal I had written in the past, illustrating how I approached complex narratives and budget justifications. A few months later, I received a rather unexpected call from a longtime contact and program officer at the Department of Corrections.

She said, "David, we just received a proposal from another agency—but it reads *exactly* like something you would have written." She was undeniably right. The organization had taken my example, changed only a few superficial specifics, and submitted it as their own, unique work. The department, recognizing the nearly identical language and structure, rejected it outright, explicitly citing serious ethical concerns.

That defining moment stayed with me, profoundly shaping my approach to grant writing and teaching. It taught me that ethical breaches in grant writing are not always born of malicious intent—often, they stem from ignorance, immense pressure, or a misunderstanding of professional boundaries—but they are consistently and severely **consequential**. They erode the most fundamental currency in grantmaking: **trust**. And in the world of philanthropy, grantmaking, and public funding, trust is, quite simply, everything.

Grant writing is not simply a technical skill; it is, at its core, an **act of trust**. Funders rely absolutely on proposals to understand the genuine truth of a problem, the authentic capacity of an organization, and the unquestionable credibility of a proposed solution. Every carefully crafted sentence, every verifiable statistic, and every line item in a budget carries immense weight and responsibility. That is precisely why ethics, integrity, and unwavering responsibility must remain at the very heart of every grant development effort, from the earliest conceptualization to the final report.

In my decades as both a grant writer and a meticulous reviewer, I've observed firsthand how the **intense demands of the funding landscape** often create immense pressure on organizations. With **budgets consistently stretched thin and the imperative for measurable impact ever-increasing**, the temptation to stretch the truth—to overpromise outcomes, to inflate needs or impact data, or to unethically reuse content—is a very real, pervasive challenge. Yet, yielding to these short-term choices can inevitably lead to devastating long-term consequences: irrevocably damaged organizational reputations, permanently fractured funder relationships, or even severe legal and compliance implications. Ethical grant writing is not just about avoiding punishment; it's about building sustainable impact and long-term partnerships.

The Temptation to Overpromise: Realistic Goals, Credible Impact

One of the most common and damaging ethical missteps in grant writing is the impulse to promise more than a program can realistically and credibly deliver. Grant writers, driven by enthusiasm or desperation, naturally want to impress funders. They strive for their proposal to stand out, to paint the most optimistic picture possible. But when proposed outcomes are exaggerated, timelines are overly ambitious, or the capacity to deliver is overstated, it not only sets the organization up for inevitable failure and disappointment during implementation—it fundamentally undermines the credibility of the entire nonprofit and public service sector. Funders, after all, share information and track performance.

The most ethical proposals are paradoxically also the most strategic: they are deeply rooted in a clear, honest understanding of their organization's genuine capacity, the real-world context in which the program will operate, and the realistic scale of achievable impact. They meticulously describe what **can** truly be accomplished with the requested resources, not merely what would look impressive or aspirational on paper.

Best Practices to Counter Overpromising:

- **Anchor to Data:** Ground all claims in verifiable data, past performance, or established research. If you project a 20% increase in client outcomes, explain how you've achieved similar results before or cite studies that support your methodology.

- **Consult Program Staff:** Engage program managers and direct service staff who intimately understand daily operations. They can provide realistic assessments of what's achievable with the given resources and within the proposed timeline.

- **Define SMART Objectives:** Ensure all objectives are **S**pecific, **M**easurable, **A**chievable, **R**elevant, and **T**ime-bound. This framework naturally builds in realism.

- **Acknowledge Challenges (Proactively):** Ethically, it's often more credible to briefly acknowledge potential challenges or risks and how your organization plans to mitigate them, rather than presenting a flawless, unrealistic scenario. This demonstrates foresight and preparedness.

Copy-and-Paste Syndrome: The Perils of Uncritical Reuse

The practice of recycling proposals—or significant portions of them—without meticulous tailoring to a new funder's unique priorities, guidelines, or values is far more than just lazy; it is profoundly misleading and unprofessional. A beautifully crafted proposal written for a corporate foundation with a focus on employee volunteerism, for example, may bear little relevance or alignment with the rigorous, compliance-heavy expectations of a federal agency focused on scientific research. Submitting reused content without deep adaptation and contextualization inevitably results in wasted time for both the applicant (who almost certainly receives a rejection) and the reviewer (who must sift through irrelevant material). At worst, it can be perceived as disrespectful or a sign of a lack of genuine interest in the funder's mission.

Ethical grant writers treat each proposal as a **bespoke communication**—a unique opportunity to articulate their vision in a way that resonates specifically with the prospective funder. Even when core organizational or program content is reused, it absolutely must be updated, meticulously contextualized, and made fully relevant to the new audience, their specific priorities, and the particular funding opportunity.

Coming from an academic background, I often reflect on the rigorous practice of self-citation in scholarly publishing. In academic contexts, authors are explicitly expected to cite their own previous work if they reuse material, even when they are the sole author. While grant writing does not typically require formal academic citation in the same way, there is still a clear professional and ethical expectation to avoid recycling content indiscriminately or without careful thought. Copying wholesale from previous proposals without critical review often leads to intellectual laziness, overlooks the distinctiveness of the new funding opportunity, and risks producing a submission that feels out of sync with the funder's specific mission or the current context. At its core, good, ethical grant writing is about **relevance and authentic engagement**—and recycled content, no matter how polished in its original form, can quickly become irrelevant and undermine the proposal's integrity.

Strategies to Avoid "Copy-and-Paste Syndrome":

- **Start with the Funder:** Always begin your proposal development by dissecting the funder's guidelines, mission, and past giving patterns. Let *their* priorities shape *your* narrative.

- **Create a Core Content Library, Not a Template:** Instead of reusing old proposals as templates, develop a library of core organizational descriptions, program models, and impact data. This allows you to pull accurate, up-to-date information but always forces you to re-assemble and adapt it for each unique application.

- **Contextualize Everything:** Every statistic, every program description, every outcome should be framed within the context of the specific funder's interests and the unique opportunity.

- **Develop a "Red Team" Review:** Have someone unfamiliar with the previous proposal read the "recycled" one to see if it truly speaks to the new funder's context.

Budgets That Stretch the Truth: Financial Integrity

A grant proposal's budget is far more than a mere list of numbers; it tells a crucial story—the financial narrative of your proposed project. When that story doesn't logically match the narrative portion of the proposal, or worse, when costs are deliberately hidden, unrealistically inflated, or deceptively presented, it immediately raises significant red flags for astute reviewers. Practices such as artificially underestimating costs to appear more competitive or intentionally overbudgeting to secure surplus funds are both serious ethical breaches that profoundly erode trust and can lead to immediate disqualification.

Ethical budgeting demands:

- **Aligning Every Expense with a Clear Activity:** Every dollar requested should directly support a specific, identifiable program activity or organizational need described in the narrative. There should be no "fluff" or unexplained line items. Funders often cross-reference the budget with the narrative to ensure consistency.

- **Justifying Costs Based on Real Data:** All cost estimates should be grounded in reality—based on recent quotes from vendors, historical expenditure data, or current market rates. Avoid arbitrary numbers. For personnel, use actual salary scales and benefits rates. For equipment, get legitimate vendor quotes.

- **Transparently Including In-Kind or Matching Contributions:** If your organization or partners are contributing resources (volunteer time, donated space, existing staff salaries) that are not cash but support the project, transparently include these "in-kind" contributions and explain their valuation. This demonstrates commitment and leverages the grant funds, but they must be clearly identified as non-cash.

- **Adhering to GAAP (Generally Accepted Accounting Principles):** For larger grants, especially federal ones, adherence to professional accounting standards is expected. Ethical budgeting implies financial systems that can accurately track and report expenditures.

Authorship and Attribution: Ownership and Accountability

In many contemporary organizations, grant proposals are inherently collaborative team efforts. Program staff, finance directors, evaluation specialists, external consultants, and executive leadership may all contribute significant sections or provide critical data. Transparency about authorship—especially when external writers or consultants are utilized—is not just a best practice; it's fundamental to internal accountability and external credibility. Not because funders necessarily need to know every individual hand involved, but because clear communication within the organization ensures that the content accurately reflects the organization's real plans, capacity, and collective voice.

If someone is **ghostwriting** a grant—meaning they are writing the primary narrative without being publicly credited—there must be robust internal systems in place to ensure the content genuinely reflects the organization's actual plans, demonstrated capacity, and authentic voice. Misrepresentation—whether intentional or unintentional—can easily result when too much creative control is outsourced without adequate internal oversight and collaborative review.

A particularly sensitive related concern involves the use of **external grant writing consultants**. While many consultants bring invaluable expertise, efficiency, and a fresh perspective, there is an inherent ethical tension when they work across multiple clients who may be competing for similar funding opportunities, especially within the same geographic or programmatic space. The risk of inadvertently or even intentionally "borrowing" compelling narrative elements, efficient budget language, or even program designs from one client to bolster another can profoundly erode trust, create serious conflicts of interest, and compromise the unique vision of each organization.

Organizations that choose to rely on consultants should establish clear, legally binding expectations and ethical boundaries from the outset. Agreements should meticulously cover:

- **Confidentiality:** Strict clauses regarding client information.
- **Ownership of Content:** Clearly define who owns the intellectual property of the generated content (typically the client organization).
- **Disclosure of Potential Overlaps:** Require the consultant to disclose any other clients they are working with on similar opportunities to identify and manage potential conflicts of interest.
- **Avoiding Conflicts:** Establish guidelines for whether the consultant can work with direct competitors or apply for the exact same funding opportunity for multiple clients.

Just as importantly, internal staff should stay actively and substantively involved throughout the entire proposal development process. This ensures that proposals genuinely reflect the organization's authentic voice, unique mission, and strategic direction—not just a consultant's generic template, recycled content, or a "flavor of the month" approach. It is *your* story to tell.

Reporting: The Fulfillment of the Promise and Sustaining Trust

The ethical obligations inherent in grant writing certainly don't end when the proposal is submitted—or even when the eagerly awaited grant award notification arrives. **Reporting on how funds were used and what impact was achieved is a critical, ongoing component of ethical stewardship.** It is, quite literally, the fulfillment of the promise meticulously made in the application.

Too often, reporting is regrettably treated as a burdensome compliance chore, an administrative hoop to jump through. But timely, accurate, and deeply reflective reporting is, in fact, one of the most powerful tools for building and sustaining long-term trust with funders, clearly demonstrating your organization's profound impact, and laying the essential groundwork for continued investment in its mission.

Funders are seasoned professionals; they understand that not every aspect of a complex program goes perfectly according to the initial plan. What truly matters to them is **honesty, adaptability, and a genuine willingness to share both successes and the hard-won lessons learned.** Ethical reporting encompasses:

- **Acknowledging Challenges and Delays:** Be transparent about any significant challenges encountered, delays in timelines, or unforeseen obstacles. Explain *why* they occurred and *how* your organization is addressing them. This demonstrates accountability and problem-solving.

- **Updating Outcomes Based on Real Data:** Report on actual outcomes and impacts using real, verified data, even if they differ slightly from initial projections. If an outcome was not met, explain why and what adjustments were made. Data integrity is paramount.

- **Providing Comprehensive Documentation of Expenditures:** Ensure all financial reports are accurate, reconcile with your accounting records, and are accompanied by necessary documentation as required by the grant agreement. Fiscal transparency builds immense confidence.

- **Sharing Qualitative Impact:** Beyond numbers, share compelling stories, testimonials, or anecdotal evidence that illustrate the human impact of your work, consistent with the data.

Conclusion: Integrity Is a Competitive Advantage

In today's intensely competitive funding landscape, integrity might sometimes seem like a "soft skill" or an abstract ideal. However, it is, in reality, a profound and sustainable competitive advantage. Funders are a tight-knit community; they communicate. They remember. Organizations known for unwavering transparency, consistent follow-through on promises, meticulous stewardship of funds, and impeccably ethical grant management are not only more likely to be successful in current applications but are often proactively invited back to apply again for future opportunities. They become preferred partners.

Ethics in grant writing is not about striving for an impossible perfection. It's about **uncompromising alignment.** It's about diligently ensuring that what you boldly propose in your application, what you meticulously fund with awarded resources, and what you honestly report on as impact are all part of the same truthful, consistent, and credible story.

As you move forward in your transformative grant writing journey, let integrity be your fundamental baseline—your guiding principle in every decision—rather than a mere afterthought. This commitment will not only serve your organization well but will also strengthen the entire philanthropic ecosystem.

References

Bill & Melinda Gates Foundation. (n.d.). Retrieved from https://www.gatesfoundation.org

Carnegie, A. (1889). The gospel of wealth. *North American Review, 148*(391), 653–664.

GrantCraft. (2010). *Working with evaluators: A guide for nonprofits*. Retrieved from https://grantcraft.org/content/guides/working-with-evaluators/

Grants.gov. (n.d.). Retrieved from https://www.grants.gov

Grønbjerg, K. A. (1993). *Understanding nonprofit funding: Managing revenues in social services and community development organizations*. Jossey-Bass.

Knowlton, L. W., & Phillips, C. C. (2013). *The logic model guidebook: Better strategies for great results* (2nd ed.). SAGE.

Maurrasse, D. J. (2020). *Philanthropy and society*. Polity Press.

Murray, D. L., Morris, D., Lavoie, C., Leavitt, P. R., MacIsaac, H., Masson, M. E., ... & Taylor, N. (2016). Bias in research grant evaluation has dire consequences for small universities. *PLOS ONE, 11*(6), e0155876. https://doi.org/10.1371/journal.pone.0155876

New Philanthropy Capital. (2014). *Theory of change: The beginning of making a difference*. Retrieved from https://www.thinknpc.org/resource-hub/theory-of-change/

Parks, E. J., & Kaufman, R. (2011). *Effective grant writing and program evaluation for human service professionals*. Springer Publishing Company.

Renfro, A. M. (2024). *Grant writing: The essentials* (2nd ed.). Jossey-Bass.

Rossi, P. H., Lipsey, M. W., & Freeman, H. E. (2004). *Evaluation: A systematic approach* (7th ed.). SAGE.

Salamon, L. M. (2012). *The resilient sector: The state of nonprofit America*. Brookings Institution Press.

W.K. Kellogg Foundation. (2004). *Logic model development guide*. Retrieved from https://www.wkkf.org/resource-directory/resources/2004/01/logic-model-development-guide

Appendix A: Grant Feasibility Study Worksheet

How to Use This Worksheet

This Grant Feasibility Study Worksheet is designed to help you assess whether your organization is ready to pursue a particular funding opportunity. It works best when used early in the planning process—before you begin drafting the full proposal. You can complete it individually, as a leadership team, or collaboratively with potential partners.

For each item, check "Yes," "No," or "Not Sure." Use the responses to identify areas of strength and areas that may require further development, discussion, or capacity-building. A "No" or "Not Sure" response doesn't mean you can't move forward—it signals where you may need to gather more information or strengthen internal readiness.

Section 1: Organizational Readiness

1. Does your organization have the capacity (staff, infrastructure, experience) to carry out this project?
[ ] Yes   [ ] No   [ ] Not Sure

2. Have you successfully managed a grant of this size and scope before?
[ ] Yes   [ ] No   [ ] Not Sure

3. Do you have systems in place for fiscal management, reporting, and compliance?
[ ] Yes   [ ] No   [ ] Not Sure

Section 2: Strategic Alignment

4. Is the proposed project aligned with your organization's mission and strategic goals?
[ ] Yes   [ ] No   [ ] Not Sure

5. Does the project clearly respond to a documented need in your community or field?
[ ] Yes   [ ] No   [ ] Not Sure

6. Is this the right time to undertake this project?
[ ] Yes   [ ] No   [ ] Not Sure

Section 3: Funder Fit

7. Have you reviewed the funder's guidelines and eligibility requirements thoroughly?
[ ] Yes   [ ] No   [ ] Not Sure

8. Does your project clearly align with the funder's priorities and focus areas?
[ ] Yes   [ ] No   [ ] Not Sure

9. Have you reviewed previously funded projects to ensure alignment?
[ ] Yes   [ ] No   [ ] Not Sure

Section 4: Project Clarity

10. Are your goals, objectives, and outcomes clearly defined and measurable?
[ ] Yes   [ ] No   [ ] Not Sure

11. Do you have a preliminary project timeline and staffing plan?
[ ] Yes   [ ] No   [ ] Not Sure

12. Have you considered how you will evaluate success?
[ ] Yes   [ ] No   [ ] Not Sure

Section 5: Budget Readiness

13. Have you drafted a sources and uses budget for the project?
[ ] Yes   [ ] No   [ ] Not Sure

14. Do you have cost estimates or quotes for major expenses?
[ ] Yes   [ ] No   [ ] Not Sure

15. Will your organization or partners provide in-kind or matching resources?
[ ] Yes   [ ] No   [ ] Not Sure

Section 6: Partnerships and Stakeholders

16. Are necessary partners or collaborators already engaged?
[ ] Yes   [ ] No   [ ] Not Sure

17. Have you clearly defined each partner's role in the project?
[ ] Yes   [ ] No   [ ] Not Sure

18. Do stakeholders (e.g., clients, community members) support this initiative?
[ ] Yes   [ ] No   [ ] Not Sure

Section 7: Risk Readiness

19. Have you identified any major risks to project success?
[ ] Yes   [ ] No   [ ] Not Sure

20. Do you have contingency plans for staffing, funding, or timeline delays?
[ ] Yes   [ ] No   [ ] Not Sure

Appendix B: Logic Model Template and Sample

A logic model is a visual planning tool that links your program's resources and activities to its intended outcomes. Funders often request a logic model to assess program coherence and feasibility. This appendix includes both a blank template and a completed sample.

Part 1: Logic Model Template

Use this blank table to define your program components. Logic models often follow this left-to-right flow:

Inputs	Activities	Outputs	Short-Term Outcomes	Long-Term Outcomes

Part 2: Sample Logic Model – Youth Mentorship Program

This example demonstrates how to map out a school-based mentorship program.

Inputs	Activities	Outputs	Short-Term Outcomes	Long-Term Outcomes
Grant funding Staff time School facilities Partner organizations	Weekly mentorship sessions Family workshops Field trips	60 mentoring sessions held 100 students enrolled 3 family events hosted	Improved attendance Higher homework completion Increased engagement	Higher graduation rates Improved academic performance Greater college enrollment

Appendix C: Sample Sources and Uses Budget (Detailed Allocation)

This table illustrates a complete **Sources and Uses Budget**, a highly transparent format that delineates all anticipated revenues (Sources) and precisely how each expenditure (Use) is funded. Notice how the total for each "Use" line is distributed across the "Source" columns, ensuring all funds are accounted for and balanced.

Expense Category	Total Cost	XYZ Foundation Grant	of Anytown Matching Fu	In-Kind Contributions
Program Manager (0.75 FTE)	60000	40000	20000	0
Outreach Worker (0.5 FTE)	30000	20000	10000	0
Fringe Benefits (25%)	22500	15000	7500	0
Supplies and Equipment	10000	10000	0	0
Printing & Outreach Materials	5000	5000	0	0
Facility Use (In-Kind)	20000	0	0	20000
TOTAL	147500	90000	37500	20000

Sample Sources and Uses Budget Narrative

This Budget Narrative provides a detailed justification for the expenditures outlined in the accompanying Sources and Uses Budget table. It explains the necessity and calculation of each line item, demonstrating how resources are strategically allocated across various funding streams to achieve the program's objectives.

Personnel

Program Manager (0.75 FTE): This line item covers 75% of the Program Manager's time (30 hours/week) for 12 months, at an annual salary of $80,000. This role is essential for strategic oversight, grant compliance, coordination with partners, and reporting as detailed in the Program Description. The cost is distributed across the XYZ Foundation Grant ($40,000) and the City of Anytown Matching Funds ($20,000), demonstrating leveraged investment. Total cost: $60,000.

Outreach Worker (0.5 FTE): This expense covers 50% of the Outreach Worker's time (20 hours/week) for 12 months, at an annual salary of $60,000. This staff member will be responsible for participant recruitment, facilitation of outreach events, and frontline community engagement. This cost is covered through the XYZ Foundation Grant ($20,000) and City of Anytown Matching Funds ($10,000). Total cost: $30,000.

Fringe Benefits (25%)

Fringe Benefits: Fringe benefits are calculated at 25% of total personnel costs ($90,000), resulting in a total of $22,500. This includes FICA, health and dental insurance, unemployment insurance, and retirement contributions. The benefits are allocated to the XYZ Foundation Grant ($15,000) and the City of Anytown Matching Funds ($7,500).

Operations

Supplies and Equipment: This item covers program materials, office supplies, and basic technology necessary for delivery of services. The entire cost of $10,000 is funded through the XYZ Foundation Grant.

Printing & Outreach Materials: Printing costs include outreach flyers, enrollment forms, and training manuals for participants. All $5,000 of this cost is funded by the XYZ Foundation Grant.

Facility Use (In-Kind): Use of donated meeting space for workshops and staff operations is valued at $20,000. This in-kind contribution is provided by a community partner at no cost to the program.

Appendix D: Budget Justification Checklist

This checklist provides a systematic guide for developing a comprehensive and transparent budget narrative. It ensures that every line item in your numeric budget (as outlined in Chapter 4) is clearly justified, explained, and aligned with your proposed program activities and objectives. Use this tool to articulate the financial story of your project and build funder confidence.

Section 1: General Justification Principles

- [ ] **Clarity & Conciseness:** Is the language clear, direct, and easy to understand? Is it free of jargon?

- [ ] **Alignment with Narrative:** Does every budget item directly relate to an activity or outcome described in the project narrative (Chapter 3)?

- [ ] **Justification for Each Item:** Is there a clear explanation for *why* each cost is necessary?

- [ ] **Transparency in Calculation:** Are all calculations (e.g., FTEs, hourly rates, unit costs) clearly shown and easily verifiable?

- [ ] **Consistency:** Are the figures consistent with the numeric budget table?

- [ ] **Relevance:** Is every item essential for the successful implementation of the proposed project?

- [ ] **No Unallowable Costs:** Have all expenses been screened against funder guidelines for unallowable costs (Chapter 4)?

Section 2: Personnel Costs Justification

- [ ] **Position Title:** Is the full title of each position clearly stated?

- [ ] **Role & Responsibilities:** Is a brief but clear description of each individual's (or position's) specific duties *related to this project* provided?

- [ ] **Time Commitment:** Is the percentage of Full-Time Equivalent (FTE) or hours per week dedicated to the project clearly indicated?
- [ ] **Salary/Wage Rate:** Is the annual salary or hourly wage rate clearly stated?
- [ ] **Calculation:** Is the calculation for the requested amount shown (e.g., FTE x annual salary = total requested)?
- [ ] **Existing vs. New Hire:** Is it clear whether this is an existing staff member allocating time or a new position?
- [ ] **Total Personnel Cost:** Does the sum match the numeric budget?

Section 3: Fringe Benefits Justification

- [ ] **Rate & Calculation:** Is the fringe benefit rate (e.g., as a percentage of salaries) clearly stated and calculated?
- [ ] **Components:** Is it clear what the fringe benefits include (e.g., health insurance, retirement, FICA, unemployment, workers' comp)?
- [ ] **Alignment:** Is the fringe benefit amount consistent with the personnel costs?

Section 4: Equipment & Supplies Justification

- [ ] **Itemized List:** Are all major equipment pieces and significant supply categories itemized?
- [ ] **Unit Cost & Quantity:** Is the unit cost and quantity for each item provided?
- [ ] **Purpose:** Is the direct relevance and necessity of each item to project activities clearly justified?
    - *Example: "10 tablets @ $300/each = $3,000 for participant data collection during intake sessions, as outlined in the Evaluation Plan."*

Section 5: Travel Justification

- [ ] **Purpose of Travel:** Is the purpose of all travel (e.g., staff training, participant transport, site visits) clearly explained?
- [ ] **Travelers:** Who will be traveling (staff, participants)?
- [ ] **Destinations/Mileage:** Is the destination or estimated mileage provided?
- [ ] **Cost Breakdown:** Are costs itemized (e.g., airfare, lodging, per diem, mileage rate) and calculated clearly?

Section 6: Contractual/Consultant Services Justification

- [ ] **Provider & Role:** Is the name (if known) or type of consultant/contractor (e.g., External Evaluator, IT Consultant) and their specific role in the project identified?
- [ ] **Scope of Work:** Is a brief description of the services they will provide (deliverables) included?
- [ ] **Basis of Cost:** Is the hourly/daily rate and estimated hours/days, or fixed fee, provided?
- [ ] **Qualifications (if significant):** Are relevant qualifications briefly noted if they add credibility?

Section 7: Other Direct Costs Justification

- [ ] **Itemized List:** Are all other significant direct costs itemized (e.g., facility rental, printing, communication, utilities directly tied to project space)?
- [ ] **Calculation & Purpose:** Is the cost breakdown and direct relevance to project activities clearly justified for each item?

Section 8: Indirect Costs Justification

- [ ] **Rate Applied:** Is the specific indirect cost rate (e.g., federally negotiated, de minimis 10%, restricted funder rate) clearly stated?

- [ ] **Base:** Is the cost base to which the rate is applied identified (e.g., Total Direct Costs, Modified Total Direct Costs)?

- [ ] **Calculation:** Is the calculation for the requested indirect amount shown?

- [ ] **Policy Adherence:** Does the request adhere strictly to the funder's indirect cost policy (Chapter 4)?

Section 9: Cost-Share/Matching Justification (if applicable)

- [ ] **Source:** Is the source of the match (e.g., organizational cash, partner contribution, volunteer hours) clearly identified?

- [ ] **Type & Value:** Is it clearly identified as cash or in-kind, and is its quantifiable value provided?

- [ ] **Documentation:** Is the method for valuing in-kind contributions explained (e.g., independent sector volunteer rates, fair market rental value)?

- [ ] **Role:** How does this match directly support the project activities and demonstrate commitment?

Appendix E: Evaluation Planning Worksheet

How to Use This Worksheet

This **Evaluation Planning Worksheet** is designed as a practical, step-by-step guide to help you develop a clear, comprehensive, and actionable evaluation plan for your proposed program. Drawing directly from the principles discussed in Chapter 5, it prompts you to think systematically about every aspect of measuring success, demonstrating accountability, and fostering continuous program improvement. Use it to map out your evaluation's purpose, key questions, precise indicators, appropriate data sources, defined responsibilities, and realistic timelines. This tool is designed to support both **formative (ongoing during implementation)** and **summative (end-of-project/impact-focused)** evaluation efforts.

Section 1: Evaluation Purpose and Scope

Understanding the fundamental "why" of your evaluation is the crucial first step in shaping its design.

1. What are the primary **goals of your evaluation**? (e.g., To assess program effectiveness, to inform program improvement, to demonstrate impact to funders, to contribute to the evidence base).

2. What specific **evaluation questions** are you trying to answer? (These should align directly with your program's goals and objectives.)

    o *Examples:* Did the program achieve its intended outcomes? How effectively was the program implemented? What are the long-term impacts of the intervention?

3. Who are the **primary audiences** for your evaluation findings? (e.g., Funders, internal leadership, program staff, beneficiaries, community stakeholders, policymakers).

4. How do you intend for the **evaluation findings to be used**? (e.g., To make decisions about program scaling, to secure future funding, to refine program activities, to inform policy advocacy).

5. Will your evaluation primarily be **formative**, **summative**, or a **blend of both**? Briefly explain why.

6. What is the overall **scope** of this evaluation? (e.g., Focused on a specific program component, a pilot program, or the entire organization).

Section 2: Goals, Objectives, and Indicators

This section connects your program's intended results to measurable signs of progress and success. (Refer to Chapter 3 for detailed guidance on Goals, Objectives, Outcomes, and Impacts - GOII.)

1. List the **specific goals of your program** as defined in your proposal. (Broad, aspirational statements).

2. For each goal, list its corresponding **SMART objectives**. Ensure each objective is:

    - **S**pecific
    - **M**easurable
    - **A**chievable
    - **R**elevant
    - **T**ime-bound

3. For each objective, identify the **key indicators** you will use to track progress or success.

    - **Process Indicators:** (Measure activities/outputs) - e.g., Number of participants served, workshops delivered.

- **Outcome Indicators:** (Measure changes in participants/systems) - e.g., % increase in knowledge, % reduction in illness-related absences.
- **Impact Indicators:** (Measure long-term, broader effects) - e.g., Changes in community health indices, policy adoption.

4. What is your **baseline data** for each key indicator? Where will this baseline come from?

5. What are your **benchmarks or targets** for each indicator? (e.g., "75% of participants will demonstrate X by Y date").

Section 3: Data Collection and Sources

This section outlines the practical "how" of gathering the information needed for your evaluation. (Refer to Chapter 5 for comprehensive methodologies.)

1. What **methodologies** will you employ? (e.g., Quantitative, Qualitative, Mixed Methods).

2. What specific **data collection methods and tools** will you use for each indicator?
   - *Quantitative Methods:* (e.g., Surveys, Pre/Post Tests, Administrative Data Review, Performance Tracking, Health Records analysis).
   - *Qualitative Methods:* (e.g., In-depth Interviews, Focus Groups, Observations, Case Studies, Open-ended Survey Questions).

3. Who will be the **primary source of data**? (e.g., Program participants, staff, parents/guardians, community partners, external databases).

4. How **frequently** will data be collected for each indicator? (e.g., Weekly, monthly, quarterly, at intake, at program completion, 6-month follow-up).

5. How will you ensure **data quality and accuracy**? (e.g., Training for data collectors, data validation procedures).

6. What **ethical considerations** will guide your data collection? (e.g., Informed consent, confidentiality/anonymity, data security and storage).

Section 4: Evaluation Roles and Timeline

Clearly defining who is responsible for evaluation and when activities will occur is vital for successful execution.

1. Who will **conduct the evaluation**? (e.g., Internal staff, external evaluator, a collaborative team).
   - If internal, specify roles (e.g., Project Manager, Program Staff, dedicated Data Analyst).
   - If external, briefly describe their qualifications/expertise.

2. What are the **specific responsibilities** of each person/entity involved in the evaluation? (e.g., Data collection, data entry, analysis, report writing).

3. What is the **timeline for key evaluation activities**? (Outline major milestones, such as baseline data collection, mid-point reviews, final data collection, report drafting, and dissemination).

Evaluation Activity	Responsible Party	Timeline/Due Date
Design/Refine Evaluation Plan		
Baseline Data Collection		
Formative Data Collection		
Mid-Point Review/Report		
Summative Data Collection		

Evaluation Activity	Responsible Party	Timeline/Due Date
Final Data Analysis		
Draft Final Evaluation Report		
Share Findings (Internal/External)		

Section 5: Budgeting and Resources

A realistic evaluation plan requires dedicated resources. (Refer to Chapter 4 for budget development guidance.)

1. Have you allocated **sufficient funds** for evaluation activities? (Typically 5–10% of the grant's total budget, depending on rigor and scope).

2. What are the estimated **costs** for each evaluation component? (e.g., Evaluator fees, survey software subscriptions, data entry, printing reports, participant incentives for evaluation).

3. What specific **tools, software, or systems** will you need to support data collection, management, and analysis? (e.g., SurveyMonkey, Qualtrics, SPSS, NVivo, a CRM system, secure data storage).

4. What **in-kind or leveraged resources** will contribute to the evaluation? (e.g., Volunteer time for data entry, donated meeting space for focus groups).

Section 6: Evaluation Reporting and Use

This section outlines how you will share your findings and ensure they lead to actionable insights.

1. Who will **receive evaluation results**? (e.g., Funders, internal leadership, program staff, board of directors, community advisory committees, general public, policymakers).

2. What **format(s)** will reports take for different audiences? (e.g., Comprehensive narrative report, executive summary, infographics, dashboards, presentations, academic papers).

3. How will you ensure that **findings genuinely inform program decisions** and contribute to continuous improvement going forward? (e.g., Dedicated debrief meetings, integration into strategic planning, policy advocacy).

4. What is your plan for **disseminating findings** to a broader audience (if applicable)? (e.g., Website publication, conference presentations, peer-reviewed articles).

Section 7: Sample Formative and Summative Evaluation Questions

These are example questions to guide your thinking. Adapt them to your specific program.

Formative Evaluation (Ongoing During Implementation):

- Are program activities being implemented as planned and reaching the target population as intended (fidelity and reach)?
- What are participants' immediate reactions to the program activities and materials? How satisfied are they?
- Are program staff adequately trained and supported to deliver services effectively?
- What operational challenges are arising during implementation, and how are we addressing them?
- Are milestones and timelines being met according to the project plan?
- What early insights can inform mid-course corrections to improve program delivery?
- Are resources being utilized efficiently?

Summative Evaluation (Conducted After Program Completion):

- Did the program achieve its stated objectives and intended outcomes? (e.g., Did participant knowledge increase by X%? Was there a Y% reduction in absenteeism?)
- To what extent did the program contribute to or cause the observed changes in the target population or system?
- Was the program implemented effectively and with fidelity to its design?
- What was the overall impact of the program on the target community or problem it aimed to address?
- Was the program cost-effective or cost-beneficial in achieving its results?
- What were the key successes, challenges, and lessons learned from the overall program implementation?
- What recommendations can be made for future programming, scalability, or policy implications based on the findings?
- Does the program warrant continuation, replication, or discontinuation?

Appendix F: Sample Data Collection Plan

This **Sample Data Collection Plan** provides a structured framework for systematically gathering the information needed for your program's evaluation. It helps ensure that data collection efforts are comprehensive, aligned with your evaluation questions and indicators, and assigned clear responsibilities and timelines. Use this template as a guide to tailor a plan specific to your project, ensuring consistent and reliable data acquisition.

Program/Project Name: [Insert Your Program/Project Name Here] **Grant Period:** [Start Date] – [End Date] **Evaluation Lead/Coordinator:** [Name/Title]

Section 1: Overview of Evaluation Questions & Indicators

- **Overall Evaluation Purpose:** [Briefly restate the main goal of your evaluation, e.g., "To assess the effectiveness of X program in improving Y outcomes."]

- **Key Evaluation Questions:** (List the primary questions your evaluation seeks to answer, as identified in your Evaluation Planning Worksheet - Appendix E)

    1. [Evaluation Question 1]
    2. [Evaluation Question 2]
    3. [Evaluation Question 3]
    - *(Add more as needed)*

Section 2: Detailed Data Collection Plan

For each **Evaluation Question**, define the plan for data collection:

- **Evaluation Question:** Did the program increase participant knowledge?
    - **Key Indicator(s):** Percentage increase in post-test scores (quantitative).

- o **Data Source(s):** Program participants, Pre/Post Surveys.
- o **Data Collection Method(s):** Administer pre/post surveys.
- o **Specific Tool/Instrument(s):** Knowledge Assessment Survey (Appendix [X] - *Note: Replace [X] with actual Appendix letter if you add this survey as an appendix*).
- o **Frequency of Collection:** At intake and program completion.
- o **Responsible Party:** Program Staff / Evaluator.
- o **Data Storage Location:** Secure online database / Encrypted drive.
- **Evaluation Question:** How satisfied are participants with program services?
    - o **Key Indicator(s):** Average satisfaction score (quantitative); Themes from open-ended comments (qualitative).
    - o **Data Source(s):** Program participants.
    - o **Data Collection Method(s):** Online survey with Likert scale and open-ended questions.
    - o **Specific Tool/Instrument(s):** Participant Satisfaction Survey.
    - o **Frequency of Collection:** Monthly.
    - o **Responsible Party:** Program Coordinator.
    - o **Data Storage Location:** Secure online survey platform.
- **Evaluation Question:** Was the program implemented as planned (fidelity)?

- **Key Indicator(s):** Percentage of activities delivered per curriculum (quantitative); Narrative of challenges (qualitative).
- **Data Source(s):** Program staff observations, Program activity logs.
- **Data Collection Method(s):** Observation Checklist, Staff Interviews / Debriefs.
- **Specific Tool/Instrument(s):** Fidelity Checklist (Appendix [Y] - *Note: Replace [Y] with actual Appendix letter if you add this checklist as an appendix*), Interview Protocol.
- **Frequency of Collection:** Bi-weekly observations, Monthly staff meetings.
- **Responsible Party:** Project Manager / Program Coordinator.
- **Data Storage Location:** Shared network drive / Meeting notes folder.

- **Evaluation Question:** Did the program reduce student absenteeism?
    - **Key Indicator(s):** Percentage reduction in illness-related absences (quantitative).
    - **Data Source(s):** School attendance records (SCUSD).
    - **Data Collection Method(s):** Administrative Data Review.
    - **Specific Tool/Instrument(s):** School District Data Portal.
    - **Frequency of Collection:** Quarterly.
    - **Responsible Party:** School Nurse / Data Analyst.

- o **Data Storage Location:** Secure server / Encrypted spreadsheet.
- **Evaluation Question:** What were the long-term changes in participant behavior?
  - o **Key Indicator(s):** Self-reported healthy eating habits (quantitative); Qualitative insights into behavior change (qualitative).
  - o **Data Source(s):** Program participants, Parents/Guardians.
  - o **Data Collection Method(s):** Follow-up Surveys, Focus Group Interviews.
  - o **Specific Tool/Instrument(s):** Post-Program Behavior Survey, Focus Group Protocol.
  - o **Frequency of Collection:** 3 & 6 months post-program.
  - o **Responsible Party:** External Evaluator.
  - o **Data Storage Location:** Encrypted drive / Transcripts server.
- **[Your Evaluation Question 1]**
  - o **Key Indicator(s):** [Your Indicator(s)]
  - o **Data Source(s):** [Your Data Source(s)]
  - o **Data Collection Method(s):** [Your Data Collection Method(s)]
  - o **Specific Tool/Instrument(s):** [Your Specific Tool(s)/Instrument(s)]
  - o **Frequency of Collection:** [Your Frequency]
  - o **Responsible Party:** [Your Responsible Party]
  - o **Data Storage Location:** [Your Data Storage Location]

- **[Your Evaluation Question 2]**
    - **Key Indicator(s):** [Your Indicator(s)]
    - **Data Source(s):** [Your Data Source(s)]
    - **Data Collection Method(s):** [Your Data Collection Method(s)]
    - **Specific Tool/Instrument(s):** [Your Specific Tool(s)/Instrument(s)]
    - **Frequency of Collection:** [Your Frequency]
    - **Responsible Party:** [Your Responsible Party]
    - **Data Storage Location:** [Your Data Storage Location]
- **[Your Evaluation Question 3]**
    - **Key Indicator(s):** [Your Indicator(s)]
    - **Data Source(s):** [Your Data Source(s)]
    - **Data Collection Method(s):** [Your Data Collection Method(s)]
    - **Specific Tool/Instrument(s):** [Your Specific Tool(s)/Instrument(s)]
    - **Frequency of Collection:** [Your Frequency]
    - **Responsible Party:** [Your Responsible Party]
    - **Data Storage Location:** [Your Data Storage Location] *(Add more Evaluation Questions as needed)*

Section 3: Data Quality & Ethical Considerations

- **Data Accuracy & Consistency:** How will you ensure the data collected is accurate and consistent across all collectors and

- methods? (e.g., Training for staff, data validation checks, standardized forms).

- **Privacy & Confidentiality:** What steps will be taken to protect participant privacy and maintain confidentiality? (e.g., Anonymization, secure storage, informed consent).

- **Informed Consent:** How will you obtain informed consent from all participants or their guardians for data collection?

- **Data Storage & Security:** Where and how will all collected data be securely stored (e.g., encrypted drives, password-protected databases, locked cabinets)? Who will have access?

- **Data Retention Policy:** How long will data be stored, and when/how will it be safely disposed of?

Section 4: Data Analysis and Reporting Preparation

- **Quantitative Data Analysis:** Briefly describe how quantitative data will be analyzed. (e.g., Descriptive statistics (averages, percentages), comparative analysis (t-tests), trend analysis).

- **Qualitative Data Analysis:** Briefly describe how qualitative data will be analyzed. (e.g., Thematic analysis, content analysis, coding).

- **Data Visualization:** How will data be presented to make it clear and impactful? (e.g., Charts, graphs, infographics, dashboards).

- **Reporting Schedule:** Outline internal and external reporting deadlines.

Appendix G: Outcomes Matrix Template

How to Use This Template

This **Outcomes Matrix Template** provides a structured way to map your program's logic, ensuring a clear and measurable path from your activities to your desired impacts. It helps you connect your program's goals, objectives, and activities directly to expected outcomes, specific indicators of success, and the data sources/methods you'll use for evaluation. Use this template to clarify your program's theory of change and strengthen your evaluation plan. (Refer to Chapter 3 for detailed guidance on Goals, Objectives, Outcomes, and Impacts - GOII, and Chapter 5 for comprehensive methodologies.)

Program/Project Name: [Insert Your Program/Project Name Here] **Grant Period:** [Start Date] – [End Date] **Overall Program Goal(s):** [State your broad program goal(s) here, e.g., "To improve health outcomes for underserved youth."]

Detailed Outcomes Map

For each **Program Objective**, define the activities, expected outcomes, and how you will measure them:

- **Program Objective:** By month 12, 75% of participants will demonstrate increased knowledge of healthy eating practices.
    - **Program Activities:**
        - Conduct 10 monthly nutrition workshops for participants.
        - Distribute healthy recipe guides weekly.
    - **Targeted Outcome(s):**
        - Participants will report increased confidence in meal planning.

- Participants will correctly identify 5 new healthy food swaps.
  - **Key Indicator(s):**
    - Percentage of participants reporting high confidence in meal planning (pre/post survey).
    - Average increase in knowledge assessment scores by 15%.
  - **Data Source(s):** Participant surveys (pre/post), Knowledge assessment quizzes.
  - **Data Collection Method(s):** Online/paper surveys, Quizzes administered in workshops.
  - **Responsible Party:** Program Staff / Evaluator.
- **Program Objective:** Within 6 months, participants will increase physical activity to 60 minutes/day, 4 days/week.
  - **Program Activities:**
    - Provide twice-weekly guided physical activity sessions.
    - Offer access to community recreation center passes.
  - **Targeted Outcome(s):**
    - Participants will report higher frequency of moderate-to-vigorous physical activity.
    - Participants will demonstrate improved fitness levels.
  - **Key Indicator(s):**
    - Percentage of participants reporting 60+ minutes activity 4x/week (journal/survey).

- Change in 1-mile run times (fitness assessment).
  - **Data Source(s):** Weekly participant journals, Post-program survey, Fitness assessments.
  - **Data Collection Method(s):** Self-report journals, Online surveys, Standardized fitness tests.
  - **Responsible Party:** Program Staff / External Partner.
- **[Your Program Objective 1]**
  - **Program Activities:** [Activities for Objective 1]
  - **Targeted Outcome(s):** [Expected Outcome(s) for Objective 1]
  - **Key Indicator(s):** [Indicator(s) for Outcome(s)]
  - **Data Source(s):** [Data Source(s)]
  - **Data Collection Method(s):** [Data Collection Method(s)]
  - **Responsible Party:** [Responsible Party]
- **[Your Program Objective 2]**
  - **Program Activities:** [Activities for Objective 2]
  - **Targeted Outcome(s):** [Expected Outcome(s) for Objective 2]
  - **Key Indicator(s):** [Indicator(s) for Outcome(s)]
  - **Data Source(s):** [Data Source(s)]
  - **Data Collection Method(s):** [Data Collection Method(s)]
  - **Responsible Party:** [Responsible Party]
- **[Your Program Objective 3]**
  - **Program Activities:** [Activities for Objective 3]

- **Targeted Outcome(s):** [Expected Outcome(s) for Objective 3]
- **Key Indicator(s):** [Indicator(s) for Outcome(s)]
- **Data Source(s):** [Data Source(s)]
- **Data Collection Method(s):** [Data Collection Method(s)]
- **Responsible Party:** [Responsible Party] *(Add more Program Objectives as needed, following this structure)*

Appendix H: Sample Evaluation Report Outline

How to Use This Outline

This **Sample Evaluation Report Outline** provides a standard, comprehensive structure for documenting and communicating the findings of your program evaluation. It's designed to help you organize your results clearly, compellingly, and in a way that resonates with various audiences, including funders, internal stakeholders, and the community. Use this outline as a template, adapting sections and depth as needed for your specific evaluation's purpose and audience. (Refer to Chapter 5 for detailed guidance on evaluation planning and reporting.)

Report Title: [e.g., Evaluation Report: [Your Program Name] Pilot Program - [Dates]] **Prepared For:** [e.g., The [Funder Name] Foundation, Board of Directors] **Prepared By:** [Your Organization Name] / [Evaluator's Name/Firm] **Date:** [Date of Report]

I. Executive Summary

- **Purpose:** Provide a concise, high-level overview of the entire report's key findings, conclusions, and recommendations. This is often the only section busy readers will fully consume.

- **Content:**
    - Brief introduction of the program and its primary goal.
    - Summary of key evaluation questions.
    - Highlight of the most significant findings (positive and, if applicable, challenges with solutions).
    - Overview of major conclusions.
    - Key recommendations for program improvement, sustainability, or future action.

II. Introduction

- **Purpose:** Set the stage for the report, providing context for the evaluation.

- **Content:**
    - Brief program description (mission, goals, target population).
    - Purpose of the evaluation (e.g., accountability, program improvement, learning).
    - Key evaluation questions addressed in the report.
    - Brief overview of the report's structure.

III. Program Description

- **Purpose:** Remind the reader of what the program is, serving as a quick reference.

- **Content:**
    - Program mission and goals.
    - Key objectives (SMART objectives).
    - Target population and geographic area.
    - Overview of primary activities and services delivered.
    - Program Logic Model (can be included or referenced as an appendix).

IV. Evaluation Methodology

- **Purpose:** Detail how the evaluation was conducted, ensuring transparency and demonstrating rigor.

- **Content:**

- o **Evaluation Design:** (e.g., Formative, Summative, Mixed-Methods, Pre/Post Design, Quasi-Experimental).
- o **Evaluation Questions:** Re-list the specific questions addressed.
- o **Data Collection Methods & Tools:**
  - Description of all methods used (e.g., surveys, interviews, focus groups, observation, administrative data review).
  - Specific tools/instruments (e.g., name of survey, assessment tools, interview protocols).
  - Sampling strategy (who was included, how many, how selected).
  - Data collection timeline.
- o **Data Analysis Plan:** How quantitative data was analyzed (e.g., descriptive statistics, inferential tests) and how qualitative data was analyzed (e.g., thematic analysis, content analysis).
- o **Ethical Considerations:** How participant privacy, confidentiality, and informed consent were ensured.
- o **Limitations of the Evaluation:** Acknowledge any factors that might have limited the evaluation's scope or generalizability.

V. Findings

- **Purpose:** Present the evaluation results clearly, linking back to evaluation questions and indicators. This is the longest section.
- **Structure:** Organize findings by evaluation question, program objective, or thematic area.
- **Content:**

- **Narrative Summary:** Describe findings in clear, accessible language.
- **Data Presentation:** Integrate quantitative data (e.g., charts, graphs, tables) and qualitative insights (e.g., compelling participant quotes) to illustrate key points.
- **Process Findings (if applicable, for formative evaluation):**
  - Fidelity of implementation (was program delivered as planned?).
  - Reach and participation rates.
  - Operational successes and challenges.
- **Outcome Findings (for summative/outcomes evaluation):**
  - Progress toward each objective, presenting specific indicator data.
  - Analysis of observed changes in knowledge, attitudes, behaviors, or conditions.
  - Comparison to benchmarks/targets.
- **Impact Findings (if applicable, for impact evaluation):**
  - Evidence of broader, long-term changes or contributions.

VI. Conclusions

- **Purpose:** Summarize what the evaluation determined about the program's effectiveness and impact.
- **Content:**

- Overall judgment of program success relative to its goals and objectives.
- Synthesis of key takeaways.
- Direct answers to the main evaluation questions.

VII. Recommendations

- **Purpose:** Provide actionable suggestions based on the findings and conclusions.
- **Content:**
    - Specific, practical recommendations for program improvement, modification, scaling, or continuation.
    - Recommendations for future evaluations or research.
    - Clearly link recommendations back to specific findings.

VIII. Discussion / Lessons Learned

- **Purpose:** Offer deeper insights, reflections, and broader implications of the findings.
- **Content:**
    - Discuss unexpected findings or emergent themes.
    - Reflect on what worked well and why, and what didn't work and why.
    - Broader implications for the organization, the field, or policy.
    - Opportunities for continuous quality improvement (CQI).

IX. Appendices (Report Specific)

- **Purpose:** Provide supplementary materials that support the report's findings but would clutter the main text.

- **Content:**
    - Full data tables.
    - Copies of data collection instruments (surveys, interview protocols).
    - Relevant program documents.
    - Evaluator's CV (if external).
    - Letters of consent forms.

Appendix I – Sample Proposal 1

Clean Hands: Brighter and Healthier Future Pilot Program

Abstract

The Clean Hands: Brighter and Healthier Future pilot program, implemented by First 5 Sacramento, addresses the urgent need for disease prevention in socioeconomically disadvantaged children in the Sacramento City Unified School District (SCUSD) through early childhood hand hygiene education. The 10-month school-based program will teach transitional kindergarten (TK) students proper handwashing techniques to reduce the spread of gastrointestinal and upper respiratory diseases. The pilot program will be implemented at John Still and Rosa Parks Elementary, two Title I schools in the SCUSD's Community School Model. The program targets handwashing skill development, critical handwashing times, and family and community involvement. Using interactive tools such as UV-sensitive gels, role-playing, and classroom activities with the assistance of trained teachers, school nurses, and community members, the program aims to increase student handwashing from two to six times daily by 100%, reduce illness-related absences by 10%, and increase TK students' family's awareness by 80% by the end of the program. Formative and summative evaluations will guide the implementation and help measure effectiveness. First 5 Sacramento is seeking a $71,500 grant from the Robert Wood Johnson Foundation to promote health equity and school readiness for TK students. Handwashing is an effective and sustainable disease prevention intervention that helps young children develop lifelong healthy habits that they can carry throughout their lives.

When we teach children self-care, we promote healthy habits that prevent the spread of infectious diseases and reduce the burden on healthcare, parents, and schools. By instilling lifelong healthy hand hygiene habits in early learners, the program seeks to improve health outcomes for individuals and the community in Sacramento, California.

Keywords: hand hygiene, handwashing, transitional kindergarten, disease prevention

Clean Hands: Brighter and Healthier Future Pilot Program

To understand the serious need for this pilot program, it is important to first examine the health challenges currently affecting young children in Sacramento, California.

Background

Disease prevention gives our communities an opportunity to live healthier lives. Often, vaccinations have a central role in preventing the spread of diseases. But what happens when a vaccine is not enough? This year, Sacramento County experienced the highest severity of seasonal flu since 2017/18 (Centers for Disease Control and Prevention [CDC], n.d.-a).

According to the California Department of Public Health (n.d.-b), the flu season peaked in February, with 9.4% of deaths related to respiratory diseases. Children were particularly vulnerable, as 50% of pediatric deaths nationwide from the flu occurred in healthy children with no other underlying health conditions (Laschinsky et al., 2025). The current seasonal flu vaccine was developed to target the H1N1 strain, but the predominant breakthrough cases in the 2024/25 season were the H3N2 strain (Laschinsky et al.). The vaccine gap left our community to rely on healthy habits such as sneezing into your arm, staying home when sick, or washing your hands to prevent spreading the flu (CDC, n.d.-b). Daily habits like handwashing can be strong defense mechanisms to fight diseases (Drexler, 2010); unfortunately, these skills are often not fully developed or are missing in young children's hygiene development.

First 5 Sacramento proposes to teach young children to wash their hands and develop healthy hand hygiene habits to help prevent the spread of upper respiratory and gastrointestinal diseases. We recommend implementing a school-based handwashing education pilot program as a primary strategy for disease prevention for transitional kindergarteners in two elementary schools within the Sacramento City Unified School District (SCUSD). Our collaboration with SCUSD Community Schools will provide much-needed resources in the implementation of our program, but a grant of $71,500 from the Robert Wood Johnson Foundation will significantly help us reach the program's overall funding goal of $233,974 to bring the valuable benefits of the Clean Hands: Brighter and Healthier Futures program directly to the transitional kindergarten-grade children at John Still Elementary and Rosa Parks Elementary schools during the 2026/27 academic school year. The scheduled timeframe is September 2026 to June 2027.

When our communities invest in prevention measures and health education, we encourage healthy habits to reduce overall health costs (Office of Disease Prevention and Health Promotion, n.d.). Healthy hand hygiene helps reduce the spread of diseases such as seasonal flu, colds, and pneumonia. Acting now to protect our children from preventable diseases helps reduce the burden on our healthcare system and community.

Organization History

First 5 Sacramento is a county-level government organization funded by the Children and Families Act of 1998, commonly known as the Tobacco Tax. Over the past 25 years, First 5 Sacramento has promoted children's health and wellness, early childhood education, childcare, and supported families through programs and services to enhance children's development during the first five years of life (First 5 Sacramento, n.d.). Because the brain develops rapidly, with 90% of a child's brain developing in the first five years of life, we provide child and family support services to enhance a child's growth during this critical growth time (First 5 Sacramento, n.d.). Health and education are cornerstones of our work to prepare children for the transition to school.

First 5 Sacramento's Strategic and Implementation Plan for 2024-27 is focused on four areas that include "racial equity, diversity, inclusion, and cultural responsiveness" (First 5 Sacramento, n.d., para. 2). One of our primary goals is for children to have access to health prevention services to support wellness (First 5 Sacramento). The First 5 Sacramento Commission has 14 members with expertise in early childhood development and health whom the Sacramento County Board of Supervisors selected to lead our efforts. We invest in programs that serve children and families in our community, such as the school readiness programs, ensuring children are physically healthy and socially adjusted in preparation for their transition to kindergarten (First 5 Sacramento). Our Readiness Program Planner, Lindsay Dunckel, has worked with First 5 for over twenty years with experience developing, implementing, and managing programs that support children through health education. The Clean Hands: Brighter and Healthier Future Pilot Program helps us support children in the transitional kindergarten phase and provide them with skills to develop healthy habits to carry beyond the first five years of their lives. By implementing this school-based program, we are preparing socioeconomically disadvantaged children to thrive in school through better health and wellness.

Mission

At First 5 Sacramento, we believe every child should enjoy the opportunity for health, happiness, and learning. Our mission is:

In partnership with parents, caregivers, and their communities, we seek to advance equitable, inclusive, and culturally responsive prevention and early intervention policies, systems, and practices that eliminate racial inequities, promote optimal health and development, and improve the lives of children prenatal through age five and their families. (First 5 Sacramento, n.d., para. 3)

Statement of Need

Each year thousands of children become ill or die from preventable diseases such as upper respiratory or gastrointestinal diseases (CDC, n.d.-a). Children living in disadvantaged socioeconomic settings have higher rates of illness with worse outcomes than all others (Wadhera et al., 2021). Approximately 20.3% of students in California come from disadvantaged socioeconomic backgrounds; in the Sacramento City Unified School District, 69.6% of the student population live in socioeconomically disadvantaged situations (California Department of Education [CDE], 2024). Making SCUSD students disproportionately more susceptible to illness than the state average. These factors make preventing the spread of diseases a critical goal in our community.

Disease transmission generally happens from person to person or from contact with objects that have germs (Cleveland Clinic, n.d.). Protecting children from germs is difficult, especially since young children explore the world by handling objects or sneezing and touching their eyes, nose, and mouth before washing their hands. Children can easily develop infections by transferring germs from their unwashed hands, not knowing they have come in contact with germs (Durani, 2023). In the United States, schools and daycare settings are the primary areas where diseases are transmitted among children (American Public Health Association, 2014).

Studies have demonstrated that implementing good handwashing routines can reduce the spread of upper respiratory diseases by 20% and gastrointestinal diseases by 33% (CDC, n.d.-c; Mo et al., 2022). According to the CDC (n.d.-a), teaching children to wash their hands with soap and water can be a simple and effective way to help reduce the spread of diseases. The CDC recommends handwashing during critical times throughout the day to minimize germ and bacteria transmission. These times include washing hands after using the toilet, sneezing, playing, or before eating (CDC, n.d.-b).

Implementing handwashing routines offers the added potential to improve school attendance by children experiencing fewer sick days (Khan et al., 2021). Children in the United States miss approximately 22 million school days each year due to the common cold (Pappas, 2024). SCUSD had a 25.4% rate of chronically absent children in the 2023/24 school year in grades TK through 8th (CDE, 2023). TK students in the SCUSD had an average of 16.3 missed days of school compared to 13.1 days for all other children statewide (CDE, 2023). Additionally, the kindergarten grade, which includes TK, makes up the highest group of chronic absences in the state, with 36% of students missing more than 10% of school days in a year (California School Boards Association, 2024). These statistics highlight an area that would greatly benefit from measures to reduce student sick days since approximately 88% of missed school days are due to illnesses such as colds, flu, and stomach aches (California Office of the Attorney General, n.d.).

Teaching children how to properly wash their hands early in life is important to help develop a lifetime habit (Children's Health, n.d.). Handwashing is a healthy habit that should be promoted through educational programs to help mitigate the spread of germs. However, school- based handwashing programs are lacking to support children and encourage compliance. The California Department of Education does not offer a hand hygiene educational program. First 5 Sacramento is working to fill this gap and promote disease prevention through health education programs.

We propose a handwashing pilot program at two SCUSD schools to teach transitional kindergarten students the importance of good hand hygiene and the necessary skills to improve their handwashing ability. We selected two Title I schools with a high percentage of socioeconomically disadvantaged students, John Still Elementary and Rosa Parks Elementary. Both schools are members of the first cohort of the Community School Model (CDE, n.d.-a).

Community schools are ideal partners for our handwashing educational program thanks to the parent and community effort dedicated to improving student outcomes in their educational framework (SCUSD, n.d.-a.). Additionally, these children are more susceptible to becoming ill, with worse health outcomes.

Our program, Clean Hands: Brighter and Healthier Futures, is a pilot program that will be implemented at John Still Elementary and Rosa Parks Elementary Schools. First 5 Sacramento will implement the pilot program with support from the SCUSD Health Services Department staff, registered nurses, teachers, and parents to promote this health-focused intervention and education program for SCUSD schools (SCUSD, n.d.-a). Our program proposes a 10-month hand hygiene and handwashing education program for 40 children in TK classes at John Stills Elementary and Rosa Parks Elementary schools. The program will begin in September of the 2026/27 school year.

Proposed Strategies/Methodology

Our pilot program strives to increase hand hygiene habits for TK students in both Rosa Parks and John Stills Elementary schools, which would mitigate the transmission of preventable diseases, thereby reducing the number of school absences. By teaching children to wash their hands with soap and water, we can safeguard one out of every three children from diarrhea caused by gastrointestinal disease and one out of five from upper respiratory diseases, both preventable diseases (CDC, n.d.-b). Handwashing school-based education programs for children are considered a strong tool in fighting preventable diseases (Mbakaya et al., 2017).

The 10-month program will begin in the 2026/27 school year. First 5 Sacramento will work with school nurses, teachers, and parent and community volunteers to conduct in-class workshops to engage the TK students in fun activities. They will learn to wash their hands correctly and at specific times throughout the day, such as after using the restroom, blowing their nose, coughing, or sneezing, and before and after eating. We will emphasize proper handwashing techniques as recommended by the CDC (n.d.-b), including scrubbing hands for 20 seconds with soap before rinsing clean. Each monthly class will be presented in an engaging manner that is age-appropriate for TK students to comprehend, like a song or a game. The sessions will occur monthly, and the topics will vary based on the proposed timeline shown in the Handwashing Program Outline (see Appendix A); each month has a theme, targets, and specific activities to achieve the goals and objectives of the Clean Hands: Healthier and Brighter Future program. Involving children in self-care can help create a feeling of ownership that increases adherence to new behaviors (Sharma et al., 2011).

Our program will educate teachers, parents, and community volunteers on the importance of handwashing and the benefits for students. When teachers, parents and community volunteers are made aware of the connection between preventable infectious diseases and healthy hand hygiene, attitudes towards health education improve, they learn to wash their own hands correctly, and they help promote compliance by encouraging students to continue healthy hand hygiene habits in the classroom and at home (Wu et al., 2022). Teachers, along with the school nurses and volunteers, will lead program activities. The school nurse will track all reported absences from the TK class at each school in the pilot program. This measure will help us determine the efficacy and sustainability of our program.

Our selected method is affected by age, learning environment, and time. We have targeted the four- to five-year-old age group because of the importance of early intervention in their brain development. Children in this age group move from the sensorimotor stage, where most of their cognitive abilities develop, into the preoperational stage, where they begin to develop language and behavioral skills (Amen University, 2024). This period is considered a critical time when the brain is at high plasticity, or adaptability, because of the billions of neurological connections and simple circuits built that create a foundation for the development of motor skills, behavioral control, language, memory, visual, and emotion at later stages in life (Center on the Developing Child at Harvard University, 2024).

The attention span of four- to five-year-olds ranges between 12 and 18 minutes (CNLD Testing & Therapy, n.d.). When a presentation is longer than this time, retaining the information is not likely. Presenting handwashing skills and information in class each month with activities lasting 10-15 minutes will help ensure that proper handwashing techniques become habit- forming, as the TK students will practice daily at school. Our monthly model contrasts with other presentations, such as safety drills done in large auditoriums on an annual or biannual basis, in crowds where the children can become easily distracted. The financial framework for our pilot program is outlined in the Sources and Uses Budget (see Appendix B), with more detailed information on the use of funding and its allocation in the Sources and Uses Budget Narrative (see Appendix C).

Proposed Timeline Summary of Milestones

Month	Objective	Outcome
August 2026	Pilot Program Introduction	Meet with the school to introduce and implement the pilot program.
September 2026	Personnel Training Handwashing Education Launch Baseline Documented	Train volunteers, parents, and teachers. Launch handwashing education in the classroom workshops. Document a baseline for proper handwashing techniques.
November 2026	Handwashing Evaluation	Evaluate proper handwashing techniques by the third month of pilot rollout.
February 2027	Handwashing Evaluation	Evaluate proper handwashing techniques by the sixth month of pilot rollout
June 2027	Pilot Program Conclusion	Conclude the pilot program and complete final evaluations by the tenth month of rollout.

Timeline of Major Milestones Narrative

1. Pilot program introduction and integration: Completed before the program launch in August 2026.

2. Teacher, parent, and community volunteer training: Completed before the program launch in September 2026.

3. Handwashing education: Implemented in the first month, September 2026.

4. Proper handwashing technique baseline documented: Completed by the end of the first month, September 2026.

5. Handwashing evaluation: Completed by the end of the third month, November 2026.

6. Handwashing evaluation: Completed by the end of the sixth month, February 2027.

7. Conclude program with celebration: Completed by the tenth month, June 2027.

8. Complete program evaluations: completed by the end of the tenth month, June 2027.

Alternative Approach One – Ambassador Program

An alternative method could be to assign a handwashing ambassador following the educational training to record and monitor handwashing techniques. Using a person to supervise was the focus of a pilot study completed by the University of Miami School of Medicine in which they assigned a hand hygiene ambassador to monitor entrants of their healthcare facilities, and if any patient, visitor, or staff member failed to use alcohol-based hand rub, then the ambassador would provide them with hand sanitizer before entering the building (Birnbach et al., 2020). This method may work well for adults who knowingly enter a hygienic facility and understand that they should not bring in germs from outside, but this logic may not transfer well into a TK classroom setting. For example, we would need the ambassador to be the teacher, the only adult able to administer hand sanitizer. It is also very time-consuming to administer to all students before entering the classroom, and it would not be an efficient and sustainable option because there is still the possibility of transmitting germs throughout the day when the teacher is not available.

Alternative Approach Two – Incentive Program

Another potential method to increase handwashing frequency would be to incentivize children, such as in a pilot study completed in South Africa. Burns et al. (2018) conducted a study in South Africa that provided children ages three to nine years old with HOPE SOAP. This colorful, translucent bar soap that had a toy inside; it provided them with snacks as an additional incentive for washing their hands. This successful study revealed that children changed their behaviors because they were incentivized (Burns et al.) For our program, this would not be a sustainable option because we would have to increase our budget to include purchasing, packaging, and delivering bar soaps to the children.

Additionally, in the South African study, the volunteer community workers visited the children's homes and conducted their survey in person. While our program relies on the parents' support in encouraging proper handwashing techniques at home, we also want to influence the children's behaviors away from the home because their peers can influence them in a school setting. Providing edible incentives may work, but it would also require additional time and consideration for food allergies and sanitary packaging to prevent the transmission of germs from hands to food prior to distribution; once again, relying on the teacher makes it inefficient and unsustainable.

Goals, Objectives, Outcomes, and Impacts

The following are the goals, objectives, outcomes, and impacts proposed for the pilot program.

Goals, Objectives, and Outcomes

Goal #1 - The Clean Hands: Brighter and Healthier Future pilot program's first goal is to improve TK students' hand hygiene habits at John Still Elementary School and Rosa Parks Elementary School through a monthly school-based handwashing education program. The program targets the spread of bacteria and viruses that cause gastrointestinal and upper respiratory diseases, two of the leading causes of illness and death in children under five.

- Objective #1: The first objective is for TK students to learn and understand the critical times for handwashing to prevent the spread of germs and diseases, including before eating and after using the toilet (CDC, n.d.-b), by the end of the third month of the program.

- Objective #2: The second objective is for TK students to learn proper handwashing skills, including the five essential steps:

wet, lather, scrub for 20 seconds, rinse, and dry (CDC, n.d.-b), at the end of the program's fourth month.

- Objective #3: The third objective is for TK students to increase their handwashing compliance by consistently washing their hands at school, at home, and in other settings by the end of the 10-month program.

A primary outcome of this goal is that upon completion of the program, 100% of TK students will increase the frequency of handwashing from an average of two times per day to approximately six times per day. The second outcome is for 80% of TK students' families' awareness of good hand hygiene to increase by the end of the 10-month program. The increased awareness will help foster good hand hygiene practices at home. The third outcome is that by the end of the 10-month handwashing program, there will be a 10% reduction in TK student absences due to gastrointestinal and upper respiratory illnesses tracked through their school attendance.

Goal #2 - The Clean Hands, Brighter and Healthier Future pilot program aims to establish regular handwashing practices during school sessions at John Still Elementary School and Rose Parks Elementary School for TK students. This will further emphasize the importance and benefits of good hand hygiene practices and prevent illness related to gastrointestinal and upper respiratory diseases.

- Objective #1: Starting the first month of the program, when students return to the classroom from various activities, they will practice proper handwashing before returning to their assigned seats. Activities can include but are not limited to returning to the classroom from recess or lunch, visiting the library or music room, and more.
- Objective #2: Starting the first month of the program, during class, track TK students' adherence to handwashing practice. This will promote student engagement and positive

reinforcement by consistently monitoring and encouraging proper hand hygiene.

Incorporating hand hygiene practices in the student's day-to-day class schedule sets a strong foundation for a lifelong lesson. It provides a cadence where students can develop a good routine. The first outcome is that by the end of the third month, 50% of students will practice hand hygiene at least 90% of the time. Tracking the success of each student washing their hands promotes their improved hand hygiene. Students will receive rewards and recognition for consistent handwashing practices. Teachers will use visual aids or checklists to track adherence. Tracking and positive reinforcement instill good habits of hand hygiene, resulting in improvement by the seventh month of the program. We anticipate that 75% of TK students will practice hand hygiene at least 90% of the time.

Impacts

We anticipate various positive impacts by implementing the handwashing program with TK students. First, TK students will have better overall health outcomes, thus reducing their levels of absence from school and visits to healthcare facilities. Second, TK students will develop lifelong good hand hygiene habits that will help prevent the spread of germs and bacteria to others in the classrooms, families, and communities. Finally, TK students will help normalize handwashing in their classrooms, homes, and communities, expanding the health benefits to others with whom they share space. The alignment between our goals, objectives, and intended outcomes is laid out in the Logic Model (see Appendix D), providing a visual representation of the inputs, activities, outputs, outcomes, and impacts of the program.

Evaluation Plan

The following outlines the methods that will assess the Clean Hands: Brighter and Healthier Future pilot program. The evaluation plan will be implemented by the project manager and presented to key stakeholders, including SCUSD administration, the SCUSD Community School

Advisory Committee, partner organizations, and potential funding organizations.

Intake Strategy

We will conduct an early assessment of the handwashing knowledge of parents and guardians through a survey. This early assessment survey will help determine a baseline of hand hygiene knowledge among TK families for implementation and comparison. The qualitative survey will ask questions on key concepts of handwashing and hand hygiene skills. The questions on the survey will include:

Family Handwashing Survey

The survey questions below will be asked of parents and guardians at the beginning and end of the program to gauge hand hygiene and handwashing awareness.

Please rate: (1) very, (2) likely, (3) somewhat likely, (4) not likely, (5) not at all.

1. How important is it for children to wash their hands?

1   2   3   4   5

2. How aware are you of when children should wash their hands (e.g., after using the restroom, before eating, after playing outside)?

1   2   3   4   5

3. How consistent is the handwashing routine in your home (e.g., before meals, after restroom use, after sneezing or coughing)?

1   2   3   4   5

4. Does your child have reliable access to soap and clean water at home for handwashing?

1   2   3   4   5

5. How many times a day does your child wash their hands? _____

Formative Evaluation Plan

The formative evaluation aims to monitor the pilot program's ongoing progress and make necessary adjustments to ensure the handwashing curriculum meets the expected outcome.

Evaluating the program during the implementation phase allows us to learn, emphasize improvement, and make modifications in real time (Fraser, 2025).

Key Questions & Evaluation Components

** Table excluded for saving space **

To determine whether a milestone has been met, we can assess whether handwashing has increased over a 10-month period by having the school nurse compare intake data with formal evaluations and observations over the first three- and six-month periods, suggest new improvement activities, recommend new tools of engagement, and provide additional family resources. This early three-month assessment questionnaire will establish a baseline for the handwashing team to gauge and document the current level of awareness among TK students and the community regarding proper handwashing practices. Student data will remain confidential, and all handwashing data will be anonymized.

Regarding measurable objectives, examples include the number of student participants in the TK classroom at John Still and Rosa Park Elementary schools, the percentage of participants in the TK community, and the frequency of handwashing activities. Teachers, parents, and classroom nurses track these statistics, with additional monitoring support from the TK community volunteers.

Our progress will be measured by comparing responses from the survey questionnaire stated in the formative evaluation against the objectives and expected outcomes. We can evaluate the feasibility of our targets by analyzing the data against the metrics outlined in our objectives and outcomes. The survey questions will evaluate students' and families' qualitative competency in handwashing behavior. Suppose our projected numbers were not met during the second formative evaluation. In that case, we will adjust our approach and set new expectations to ensure we reach our goals.

Summative Evaluation Plan

The summative evaluation plan aims to assess the pilot program's success in achieving its intended outcomes and provide insights for potential scaling or redesign. Upon completion of the program, this evaluation will be carried out to evaluate the results and effects on our targeted group (Fraser, 2025). The data collected for the summative evaluation will focus on the two primary goals of the pilot program, objectives, and desired outcomes.

Key Questions & Evaluation Components

** Table excluded for saving space **

Once the program has finished running its course, either through the end of the academic school year or the full implementation of hand hygiene behaviors among TK students, we will determine how successful the program was in meeting its outcomes of improving hand hygiene behaviors and reducing gastrointestinal and upper respiratory illnesses. Our primary goal is to reduce the spread of illnesses by improving hand hygiene behaviors through a structured school-based program for TK students. Although we aim to embed effective hand hygiene practices fully, we will consider the program successful if:

- 100% of TK students increase handwashing frequency from an average of two times per day to approximately six times per day.

- 80% of TK students' families demonstrate increased awareness of good hand hygiene.
- A 10% reduction in illness-related absences due to gastrointestinal and upper respiratory illnesses among TK students is observed.

After the program, teachers and volunteers will re-administer the same observation checklist and survey completed at the program's beginning and during month five. These tools will measure the following:

- Frequency and consistency of handwashing at critical times.
- Student's ability to perform proper handwashing steps (wet, lather, scrub for 20 seconds, rinse, dry).
- Family awareness and reported behavior change regarding hand hygiene practices at home.

The results will be compared with baseline data collected at the start to evaluate progress toward the program's outcomes.

Additionally, a confidential observation log will be maintained by teachers and volunteers.

Each TK student's behavior will be tracked anonymously, following all appropriate privacy protocols, and only gender and age will be documented for reporting purposes. The observation logs will record the following:

- Handwashing compliance after classroom transitions (e.g., recess, lunch).
- Participation levels and frequency of correct handwashing practices.
- Visual aid and checklist engagement.

We aim to achieve the following outcomes:

- By month three, at least 50% of TK students will be practicing hand hygiene at least 90% of the time.

- By month seven, at least 75% of TK students consistently practice hand hygiene at least 90% of the time.

Furthermore, illness-related absenteeism data will be collected from school attendance records. Comparing absentee rates before and after program implementation will provide objective evidence of the program's impact on student health. The data gathered from observation checklists, family surveys, and attendance records will be analyzed to measure the effectiveness of hand hygiene education and behavioral reinforcement strategies. Findings will be documented and presented to the school administration and potential future funding sources through an official PowerPoint report.

We will review teacher, parent, and volunteer feedback to change and improve our program for future implementations and potential expansion of Clean Hands: Healthier and Brighter Future to all SCUSD TK programs. The success of our pilot program will be demonstrated by improved health, consistent handwashing compliance, and overall improved hand hygiene awareness among the TK students and their families, ultimately benefiting the SCUSD community and beyond.

Relationship Between Evaluation and Program Goals/Outcomes

The Clean Hands: Brighter and Healthier Future pilot program utilizes formative and summative evaluations to meet the program's outcomes. Each evaluation helps us use our resources efficiently and adjust our program as needed (Fraser, 2025) to serve the TK students at John Still Elementary and Rosa Parks Elementary schools. The formative evaluation occurs at months three and six, acting as a periodical analysis to check if the program is on track to meet its organizational goals. The summative evaluation is conducted after the pilot program has ended. This evaluation is an assessment of the long-term effectiveness of the hand hygiene program.

The formative evaluation will occur throughout the program; this will assist in developing the implementation and adapting strategies as necessary. Monthly milestone tracking, bi- monthly reflection meetings, and quarterly feedback workshops provide periodical insights as to whether the program effectively meets the stated objectives and highlight where refinements may be needed. For example, suppose less than 50% of the TK students show improvement in handwashing by month three or the student's attendance does not improve. In that case, family intervention or tailored workshops may be prompted. The formative evaluation serves as a real- time feedback mechanism that can assist in pointing out areas of improvement and ensure that the program stays on track to increasing handwashing behavior among the TK student population at John Still Elementary and Rosa Parks Elementary schools.

The summative evaluation is conducted at the end of the pilot program, evaluating its outcomes and overall impact. The TK student's baseline hand hygiene knowledge is compared with the data from the pilot programs for months five and ten. The priority outcomes include increasing the frequency of handwashing habits among the TK students from two to six times per day, reducing illness-related absences by 10%, and increasing the students' family awareness by 80%. All of these key outcomes will indicate whether the curriculum of the pilot program improved hand hygiene habits and reduced illness-related absenteeism.

The formative and summative evaluations act as a form of accountability for the program.

They are tools to ensure the program aligns with their set expected outcomes. The structure of the evaluation process also helped identify what learning tools were the most effective during the course of the program. The evaluations ground the program in continuous feedback and outcome analysis, keeping Clean Hands: Brighter and Healthier Future aligned with effectively benefiting the children of John Still Elementary and Rosa Parks Elementary schools.

In summary, the Clean Hands: Brighter and Healthier Future pilot program, proposed by First 5 Sacramento, recommends a 10-month educational handwashing and hand hygiene in- class initiative to address the spread of preventable gastrointestinal and upper respiratory diseases among young children, particularly in socioeconomically disadvantaged communities in Sacramento, CA. The program serves children in transitional kindergarten grades at John Still and Rosa Parks, two Title I elementary schools in the SCUSD. The program utilizes age- appropriate and engaging in-class activities to teach children how and when to wash their hands properly with the aim to reduce the spread of diseases, decrease the rate of absenteeism, and build lifelong healthy habits.

The program's curriculum is based on developmental science by targeting the critical learning window of brain development in four- to five-year-old children to absorb and make handwashing a habit in their young lives. By involving teachers, parents, guardians, and community members in the educational process, we strive to improve health outcomes, increase school attendance rates, and better the Sacramento community through preventative health education. By investing in our community, we can help safeguard our children from preventable diseases and instill lifelong healthy habits.

References

** References excluded for saving space **

Appendix A Handwashing Program Outline

** Appendix excluded for saving space **

Appendix B Sources and Uses Budget

First 5 Sacramento Clean Hands: Brighter and Healthier Future Pilot Program		Costs	CSUSD "In Kind"	Funding Source: Robert Wood Johnson Foundation	Funding Source: Prime Therapeutics, LLC	Funding Source: California Community Schools Partnership Program (Funding)	Total
Personnel	2 Community School Specialist (.10 FTE) ($9302/yr each)	$18,604	$18,604				$18,604
	2 School Nurse (.10 FTE) ($7979/yr each)	$15,958	$15,958				$15,958
	1 Project Manager (1 FTE)	$110,000		$55,000	$55,000		$110,000
	2 TK Teachers (.20 FTE) ($13,955/yr each)	$27,909	$27,909				$27,909
	2 Parents and 2 community volunteers (3 hrs/month @ minimum wage x 10 months)	$1,980	$1,980				$1,980
	Benefits @30%	$52,335	$19,335	$16,500	$16,500		$52,335
	Total Salary and Benefits	**$226,786**	**$83,786**	**$71,500**	**$71,500**	**$0**	**$226,786**
Operating Expenses	Office Supplies	$2,000				$2,000	$2,000
	Office multifunction printer	$600				$600	$600
	IT equipment	$2,500				$2,500	$2,500
	Application license	$150				$150	$150
	Program Materials	$1,000				$1,000	$1,000
	Total Direct Costs	**$6,250**	**$0**	**$0**	**$0**	**$6,250**	**$6,250**
	Indirect Cost @15%	$938					$938
	TOTAL	**$233,974**	**$83,786**	**$71,500**	**$71,500**	**$6,250**	**$233,974**

Itemized budget data:
Office Supplies - paper, pens, printer cartridge, poster, easel, heavy weight paper
Office multifunction printer - scanner, copier and printer
IT equipment - laptop, monitors, other peripherials and mobile phone
Application license - Microsoft Suite, Microsoft Forms
Program Materials - Infection prevention tool kit, snacks
Facility rental fee - to host monthly workshops

Appendix C

Sources and Uses Budget Narrative

The budget narrative explains each line item and how the amounts were derived. See detailed guidance below.

Personnel:

- **In-Kind Community School Specialist** – The estimated salary for a community school specialist in Sacramento County is $93,000/year. The in-kind specialists will work with each school 10% of their time to support this program. They will provide insights into the school, provide key contacts, and sponsor the program.

- **In-Kind School Nurse** – The estimated salary for a school nurse in Sacramento County is $79,790. The existing school nurse at John Still and Rosa Park Elementary School will support this program 10% of the time to track absences related to gastrointestinal and upper respiratory illness.

- **Project Manager** – The estimated salary for a project manager in Sacramento County is

$110,000 with benefits. The project manager will be the primary staff to develop, launch, and support the program.

- **Transitional Kindergarten (TK) Teachers** – The TK teachers in Sacramento County average salary is $69,773. The in-kind teachers in John Still and Rosa Park Elementary school will support the Clean Hands program. They will emphasize with students the importance of proper handwashing and include activities during the class like incorporating handwashing practice after recess or lunch.

- **Parents and community volunteers** – Volunteers will support the program during the monthly Clean Hands workshop. They will help sign in students, parents, and other participants; distribute educational materials and tools; and clean up the facility, to name a few responsibilities.

- **Benefits** – Calculated at 30%. Includes health insurance, dental insurance, and mandatory benefits, including FICA, SSI, and workers' compensation.

Operating Expenses

- **Office supplies** - The office supplies will be used for educational flyers, handouts, and program posters.

- **Office multifunction printer** - The multifunction printer will be used to scan, copy, and print documents.

- **IT equipment** - laptop, monitor, and other IT peripherals will be used by the program project manager.

- **Application license** - The average Microsoft Suite is $150/year. The MS suite applications will be installed in the PM laptop.

- **Facility rental fee** - This will be used to host monthly Clean Hands workshops for students, parents, and the community.

- **Program Materials** - This infection prevention toolkit will be distributed during the program workshop. It will include germ solutions, LED black lights, activity sheets, and so much more for up to 300 people.

- **Indirect Costs** – Based on a provisional cost rate of 15% for Sacramento County (California Department of Public Health, n.d.-a).

Appendix D Logic Model

Clean Hands Program Goal
To improve the hand hygiene habits of TK students at John Still Elementary School and Rosa Parks Elementary School through a monthly school-based handwashing program and regular handwashing practices during school sessions.

Inputs	Activities	Outputs	Outcomes	Impacts
Staff: 2 Community School Specialist (.10 FTE), 2 School Nurse (.10 FTE) and 1 Project Manager (.5 FTE per school), 2 TK Teachers **Volunteers:** 2 parent and 2 community **Funding source:** 1. Robert Wood Johnson Foundation 2. Prime Therapeutics, LLC 3. California Community Schools Partnership Program	Clean Hands pilot launch Monthly hand washing education program Evaluate students in hand hygiene practice Parents survey of handwashing knowledge (pre and post pilot) In-class handwashing practices daily Peer influence on handwashing practices Student self-check on hand hygiene tracking board	Provide Hand washing toolkit Survey result of students and family on knowledge of handwashing technique Dedicated handwashing station as students enter the classroom Positive reinforcement of handwashing practices Student roster visual aids for tracking adherence of handwashing practices	50% of students will practice hand hygiene at least 90% of the time by end of 3rd month 75% of TK students will practice hand hygiene at least 90% of the time by end of 7th month 100% of students will increase the frequency of handwashing from 2X to 6X per day by end of program 80% of TK students' families' hand hygiene awareness to increase by end of the of program 10% reduction in TK student absences by end of program	TK students will have improved general health outcomes TK students will develop lifelong good hand hygiene habits TK students will help normalize handwashing in their classrooms, homes, and communities, expanding the health benefits to those they interact with.

Appendix J – Sample Proposal 2

Smart Moves - Bunche Edition Proposal

Abstract

Childhood obesity is a major health issue in the United States, especially among minority and low-income groups. In Los Angeles County, neighborhoods like Compton face significant challenges, including limited access to healthy foods, poor health education, and unsafe areas for physical activity. Partnership for a Healthier America (PHA) developed the program *Smart Moves: Bunche Edition* to address this urgent issue through an equity-focused after-school program centered on prevention. It features a three-part strategy that includes nutrition education sessions, behavior modification classes, and physical activity classes. To reinforce healthy habits at home, parents and caregivers are given resources to support lifestyle changes for the entire family. Together, these components aim to build long-term habits that support healthy weight management and overall wellness. *Smart Moves: Bunche Edition* sets measurable objectives, including increased knowledge of nutrition, improved physical activity levels, and lower BMI percentiles. Evaluation methods, such as pre- and post-program surveys, journals, and follow-up assessments at three and six months, ensure the program's impact is monitored and continuously improved. With a strong foundation in research and community collaboration, PHA is well equipped to implement this evidence-based initiative to create lasting change and improve childhood obesity in underserved communities. With funding, the program will be launched at Bunche Middle School in Compton, California, laying the groundwork for expansion across the school district.

Comprehensive Grant Proposal: Smart Moves - Bunche Edition

Background

In the United States, childhood obesity is an epidemic, with estimates of one in five children being obese (Centers for Disease Control and Prevention [CDC], 2024a). Low-income and minority communities are most at risk (Jung et al., 2024), and places children at risk for lifelong health challenges, such as diabetes, high blood pressure, coronary heart disease, stroke, cancer, and other chronic diseases (Children's Hospital Los Angeles, 2022). The national rate of childhood obesity is 19.7%, and in California, 16.3% of children are obese (State of Childhood Obesity, 2022). In Los Angeles County, childhood obesity is more prevalent than the California rate and matched by the extreme income inequalities between its wealthy neighborhoods and poor communities (Jung et al., 2024). As obesity rates have grown, these communities are affected the most by a dramatic decline in physical education in schools (Borawski et al., 2018). Also, for many families in underserved neighborhoods, access to fresh, nutritious food and safe spaces to play is not a given (Cedars-Sinai, 2019).

Stemming from Michelle Obama's passion for fighting childhood obesity and her *Let's Move!* campaign, our organization, Partnership for a Healthier America (PHA), has a long- standing history of addressing inequities like this. We invest in communities, collaborate with partners to remove barriers, and motivate charities, corporations, and cities to supply healthy food and inspire families with skills and knowledge to empower healthy habits (Partnership for a Healthier America, 2025g). With funding, our new program, *Smart Moves- Bunche Edition*, can help break the cycle by helping children move more and eat healthier.

Organizational Overview

We are a leading national nonprofit organization that collaborates with private, non- profit, and government sectors to establish a food system that promotes a better future by fighting systemic barriers to affordable, nutritious, and culturally affirming food. Our Mission Statement says: "We know that good food powers good health. That's why we're advancing equitable access to nutritious food for all in America to lead healthy lives" (Partnership for a Healthier America, 2025g).

History

In 2009, as the *Let's Move!* campaign was being designed to combat childhood obesity, discussions between the White House and organizations, such as the Robert Wood Johnson Foundation and the Alliance for a Healthier Generation, revealed the need for a national organization that could both lead change by using public and private partnerships and be responsible for holding companies accountable for implementation. Recognizing that ending the obesity crisis would require long-term planning and commitment, our organization, Partnership for a Healthier America, was established (Simon et al., 2017). Our work expands on the *Let's*

Move! campaign's pillars to create a healthy start for children by "empowering parents and caregivers, providing healthy food in schools, improving access to healthy, affordable foods, and increasing physical activity" (Partnership for a Healthier America, 2025f). At the launch of *Let's Move!* in 2010, President Barack Obama signed a mandate for an action plan, creating the White House Task Force on Childhood Obesity. Meanwhile, Mrs. Obama introduced our organization as an independent foundation to "accelerate existing efforts addressing childhood obesity and facilitate new commitments towards the national goal of solving childhood obesity within a generation" (Simon et al., 2017, *Creation of PHA and early work* section).

Capacity

For fifteen years, PHA has been dedicated to partnerships that align with the White House Task Force on Childhood Obesity Report. We have partnered with over 575 nationwide organizations and initiated projects that empower communities to form enduring, maintainable behaviors. For example, we assisted *Healthy Hunger Relief* in implementing a nutrition ranking system with a group of experts from the Robert Wood Johnson Foundation's Healthy Eating Research. Also, PHA offered technical assistance to our partners to assess the nutritional quality of their food (Partnership for a Healthier America, 2025b, Partnership for a Healthier America, 2025e). We partnered with Instacart and their *Good Food at Home* program, providing produce credits called *Fresh Funds*, successfully helping families form healthy habits (Partnership for a Healthier America, 2025c). In addition to addressing food equity, our partnerships align with the Taskforce Report to increase physical activity. Just a few of these include the Kaiser Foundation's program to walk or bike to school, housing developers who designed their buildings to be in a healthy and active environment, and the US Tennis Association, which built 5,000 child-friendly tennis courts (Simon et al., 2017).

Credibility

Our board of directors was established in March 2010, two months after Partnership for a Healthier America was formed. As consultants to the board, we appointed a Founders Committee, whose members had collaborated for years as leaders in several foundations to address the obesity epidemic (Simon et al., 2017). For over thirty years, our president and CEO has been dedicated to advancing food equity and improving community health. Our board members share a deep, collective understanding of the factors that contribute to childhood obesity, including chronic diseases, environmental issues, and policies. With decades of combined experience, they are active leaders in organizations, committees, and foundations committed to creating healthier futures for children (Partnership for a Healthier America, 2025a, Partnership for a Healthier America, 2025h).

Statement of Need

Almost fifteen million American children are obese (CDC, 2024a), and in general, over the last two decades, the prevalence of childhood obesity has risen by nearly eight percent (Emmerich & Ogden, 2024). The CDC reports that rates are higher among lower-income families, and "increased as family income decreased" (CDC, 2024a, *Family income* section). However, the issue extends much deeper, and many people experience the consequences. First, parents must cope with dietary changes, daily routines, and weight management programs (CDC, 2024c). Educators and schools must address obesity-related bullying, implement physical activity programs, and adjust school meal programs to promote healthier eating habits. It involves a comprehensive approach that includes "school nurses, parents, caregivers, and other community members" (CDC, 2024b, *Comprehensive approach* section). Because childhood obesity is associated with significant comorbidities, healthcare providers have an increased workload to treat those conditions (Styne et al., 2017). The rise in childhood obesity impacts the healthcare system as costs increase due to the treatment of obesity-related conditions. Compared to children and adolescents with normal BMIs, those who have elevated BMIs incur millions more in medical expenses (Trasande & Chatterjee, 2009). The CDC reports that obese children face greater risks of becoming obese adults and developing heart disease, diabetes, and depression or anxiety, which leads to higher rates of chronic illness, impacting workforce productivity, increased absenteeism, and higher healthcare costs for employers (CDC, 2024c).

Obese children may experience social isolation, bullying, or discrimination, which can affect their mental health and self-esteem. This, in turn, impacts their relationships with friends and classmates. The shame of excess weight contributes to binge eating, avoiding health care, decreased physical activity, and more weight gain (Pont et al., 2017). Lastly, the food and beverage industries face growing pressure to reformulate products, offer healthier options, and limit advertising of unhealthy foods targeted at children (Bussel & Brown, 2019).

Childhood obesity is a complex issue with multiple contributing factors. The environment and circumstances of "where we live, learn, work, and play can make healthy eating and getting enough physical activity difficult" (CDC, 2024c, *why it matters* section). The cost of food is an underlying cause. Approximately 83% of adults struggle with the increased prices of goods and services. In Los Angeles, over half of all households rely on government food assistance, 10% more than the national average (United States Census Bureau, 2024). Not enough effort is being made to improve the affordability and accessibility of healthy food. Just ten companies account for over $160 billion in sales and one-third of all U.S. packaged food and beverage purchases.

Despite efforts to promote healthier eating, "less than one-third of the companies' products are healthy" (Bussel & Brown, 2019, *first question* section). Sugar-sweetened beverages, like soda, are a significant source of calories and added sugars in the American diet. Regular consumption has been linked to obesity, cardiovascular health, dental cavities, asthma, poor diet quality, and poor academic achievement (Miller et al., 2016). Food deserts, often in low-income neighborhoods, face food insecurity due to limited access to grocery stores and an abundance of fast food and convenience stores (Children's Hospital Los Angeles, 2022). Research shows that greater access to chain supermarkets is linked to lower BMI, and a higher concentration of convenience stores is associated with increased rates of overweight youth (Executive Office of the President, 2009). Increased screen time reduces physical activity and increases exposure to advertisements for unhealthy foods. Research shows that watching three hours of television daily doubles the likelihood of obesity (American Psychological Association, 2010). Additional factors include a lack of green spaces, which limits the opportunities for outdoor physical activity, and the availability of organized activity programs. Moreover, safety concerns discourage outdoor activities, leading to reduced physical activity (Cedars-Sinai, 2019).

Given the complexity of factors contributing to childhood obesity, there is no single solution. However, we can take small but meaningful steps to build lifelong healthy habits that support a healthy weight (CDC, 2024c). The White House Task Force on Childhood Obesity made recommendations that our organization is equipped to support and help implement. First, parents and caregivers should have access to resources and tools to improve nutritional awareness, thereby empowering them to make healthier choices for their families. Studies show that well-planned nutrition education programs can improve eating habits (Executive Office of the President, 2009). Second, children must be more physically active.

They need at least 60 minutes of exercise or physical play every day (CDC, 2024c; Executive Office of the President, 2009).

For years, Partnership for a Healthier America has focused on initiatives that address food equity with the belief that good health is founded on nutritious food (Partnership for a Healthier America, 2025g). We partner with industry and encourage them to endorse healthier options. Our partner's commitments to address physical activity, nutrition, and obesity-related disparities are vital to our program, so we require a contract for each promise and utilize independent verifiers to evaluate their progress (Simon et al., 2017). We have reached over 55 cities across the nation (Partnership for a Healthier America, 2025d) and have made a significant impact with hundreds of partnerships (Simon et al., 2017). Our team members add to our competence and are well-equipped to complete our mission and work. They are experienced in creating fitness health education programs, designing and leading outreach efforts, using creative platforms and approaches to support healthy behaviors, and building impactful programs by collaborating with all types of organizations (Partnership for a Healthier America, 2025h).

As previously mentioned, Los Angeles County has one of the highest rates of childhood obesity (Jung et al., 2024). Because the County is so large, it is broken into eight Service Planning Areas. Service Planning Area-6 (SPA-6) is reported to be twice as poor as the rest of the County and has the highest rate of 26.5% of children being overweight (Children's Hospital Los Angeles, 2022). Within SPA-6, we identified Compton Unified School District as an ideal place to begin our program. We intend to address nutrition and exercise in an after-school setting at Bunche Middle School, so these children can learn foundational behaviors that contribute to developing lifelong habits and reduce childhood obesity rates. With your help in implementing *Smart Moves – Bunche Edition*, we can begin to make a positive impact where it is needed most.

Strategies and Methodologies

Schools are ideal for childhood obesity prevention efforts since they can embrace cost- effective in-school and after-school programs, policies, and practices (CDC, 2024b). One study suggests that the high rates of obesity could be reduced if schools resumed more frequent physical education programming during the school day, particularly in districts where regular physical education has been drastically reduced over the last decade. Strong, committed collaborations between schools and community programs can help bridge this gap (Borawski et al., 2018). The after-school environment has as much impact on children's physical activity and eating habits as the regular school day does (Executive Office of the President, 2009). Therefore, school-community partnerships offer a promising approach, one where children will continue to participate when the program is designed to be inclusive and fun (Borawski et al., 2018). To address childhood obesity in SPA-6, we are proposing a 12-week program each year from August to October at Bunche Middle School, located in Compton, California. The objective of this program will be to educate the students and parents about the importance of balanced nutrition and regular physical activity to help sustain long-term weight management. Furthermore, the program will aim to prevent further unhealthy weight gain among students by increasing awareness of healthy eating habits, behavior modifications, and encouraging regular exercise.

Smart Moves: Bunche Edition will be an after-school program that will offer nutrition education, behavioral modification, and physical activity. The educational classes will be held in the cafeteria and physical education will be in the school ground and gym. The nutrition education will consist of a 40-minute class led by Registered Dietitians and/or nutritionists with master level credentials. This class will educate students and their parents on alternative food options and understand the portion sizes to achieve long-term weight loss results, while emphasizing sustainable and healthy habits that provide results more than mere temporary changes, as usually associated with dieting. The nutrition education will alternate with the behavior modification classes each week. The behavior modification classes will also be 40 minutes long and will aim to educate students and caregivers about the triggers leading to overeating and develop healthy coping strategies to prevent such triggers. These classes will also be led by our registered dieticians who will encourage students to engage in discussions without their caregiver to promote and foster a more comfortable environment and allow them to share their experiences. Finally, the program will offer 50-minute exercise sessions twice a week to promote regular physical activity and support the weight management goals of the students.

These sessions will include activities such as flag football, dance, basketball, racing, and cycling, and will be led by trained Exercise Physiologists. The Program Coordinator will develop the weekly calendars and detailed session agendas in collaboration with dietitians. Physiologists and school staff. The program coordinator will also be responsible for tracking data, preparing necessary materials, and conducting regular check-ins with parents and staff.

While other strategies have been considered, such as implementing a school-wide campaign to eliminate soda consumption or creating community parks to encourage more physical activity, they both present some limitations. Encouraging students to stop drinking soda may provide short-term benefits; however, without education and nutritional habits, the behavior change will not last. In addition, having more green space and building parks are important; they require long-term funding and coordination for construction, maintenance, and city planning. As a result, *Smart Moves: Bunche Edition* offers an approach that directly engages students and their families while providing education and promoting behavior change. This program is not only more feasible in terms of implementation, but also more impactful in addressing the root causes of childhood obesity.

Timeline of Major Milestones

July: Onboard staff and training

August: Week 1: Participant enrollment begins

August: Week 2: Program Launches: First session of physical activity and nutrition education class begins.

August: Week 2- 12: Alternate weekly behavior modification and nutrition education classes; twice-weekly physical activity sessions.

October: Week 12: Final assessment, distribution of personalized progress report.

Goals, Objectives, Outcomes, and Impacts

One goal of the program is to educate students and parents about the importance of balanced nutrition and regular physical activity to help sustain long-term weight management. Participants will engage in three, forty-minute courses per week with professional instructor support, which consists of nutritional support and activities like flag football, dance, and basketball. To reach this goal, our objective is that by the end of the 12-week program, at least 70% of participating students and parents will demonstrate increased knowledge of balanced nutrition, healthier eating habits, and physical activity guidelines, as measured by pre- and post-program surveys and quizzes with a minimum 15% improvement in scores. See Appendix 1: Logic Model.

Another goal of the program is to prevent further unhealthy weight gain among students by encouraging regular exercise and increasing awareness of eating habits and behavior modifications. Participants will engage in instructor-led education courses that will focus on making better nutritional choices and discussing tools to create a healthier relationship with food. Our program objective is to follow that within 12 weeks of the program, at least 40% of students will report engaging in 60 minutes of physical activity at least four days per week and consuming at least three servings of fruits and vegetables daily, as tracked by weekly student journals and parent or caregiver check-ins. See Appendix 1: Logic Model.

Following the participant's program completion, we will look at the outcomes we are expecting over the course of the three and six months. The first projected outcome is that at least 60% of families (students, parents, caregivers) will report, via a follow-up survey at three and six months, that they regularly read food labels before purchasing, use nutrition tools for meal planning, (like MyPlate or other applications for meal planning) and schedule daily physical activities for their children, of at least 45 minutes. Of those students, 20% will increase their weekly physical activity by two times or more a week, from their starting point. See Appendix 1: Logic Model.

At the six months, following the program completion, we will have at least 40% of participating students self-reporting continued healthy eating and physical activity habits, in the form of a follow up behavioral survey; as well as maintaining or improving their overall Body Mass Index (BMI) percentile category - that will be tracked through voluntary data, initial program data, and through school health screenings. Of those students and participants, 15% will choose healthier snack and drink options and practice mindful eating, and less emotional eating. See Appendix 1: Logic Model.

After the 12-week course of the program is completed, we expect to measure our program impacts at the two-to-three-year mark. Anticipated impacts of our program are as follows: 70% of students and parents will score at least 20% higher on a post-program quiz assessing knowledge of reading food labels, identifying healthier food swaps, and recommended daily physical activity levels for youth. Furthermore, we would like to see an increase in the knowledge of our students. Therefore, we would like to see that at least 45% of students will continue with their learning and submit weekly journals for review. These journals will showcase the participants' involvement with at least 45 minutes of moderate to strenuous physical activity, four days a week, a daily intake of at least three servings of fruit and vegetables, and participation in at least one physical activity outside of the school weekly. This can consist of walking, a team sport, or a family activity. Moreover, 40% of students and family members who participated in the program will report an increase in consumption of fruits, vegetables, whole grains, and a reduction in sugary snacks and beverages. See Appendix 1: Logic Model.

Evaluation Protocol

Looking toward the future for our program, we based our evaluation process on providing an environment that gives every child a place to develop and grow. As a result, we strive to collaborate with the Robert Wood Johnson Foundation, whose vision aligns with our goals and objectives to overcome disparities and achieve health equity (Robert Wood Johnson Foundation, 2025). Through surveys, interviews, and observation techniques, we plan to use two main evaluation assessments, formative and summative, that measure the quantitative and qualitative data of the program.

Pre-Implementation Evaluation

We will start our evaluation process by conducting a formative evaluation one month before the academic year begins to prepare and gather statistical data to gauge the program's goals and objectives. A consent form will be sent to all registered families notifying them of the program during the upcoming school year. This valuable step will give us the family's consent to collect data to support the program. Coinciding with getting the consent forms in order, we will send out surveys with open-ended and multiple-choice questions to the parents and/or guardians to get a baseline understanding of the type of food the families consume and what activities occur when the students are not in school. This pre-survey will help us to understand where to start the education curriculum. This is one of the milestones in our program that indicates that we have begun to develop our program and are executing the plans. All the analysis of the data will primarily be done by the principal with help from the administrative staff.

Formative Evaluation: Pre-program Activity

Pre-surveys and focus groups are ways to gather information before the program and give baseline data that will be compared at the end of the program. Along with sending the pre-surveys to the parents, the first two weeks into the school year, a pre-survey and focus group with the students will take place during the physical education (PE) class. Students will be asked about their eating habits at home and with friends (in and outside of school). This survey will be given in conjunction with a survey from the school counselor and mental health professional to assess the mental and behavioral aspects around food and exercise from the student's perspective. During this time, nurses will weigh and calculate the BMI score of each student.

Parents will also receive a survey (email/mail) requesting feedback on the student and family's eating habits and what the parents would like to address around nutrition and exercise for their family.

Formative Evaluation: During Program Activity

The formative evaluation will continue at the 4–6-week benchmark. Since school staff interact and see more student interaction than the administrative staff, we want to have a mid- program group meeting with the staff to get their input on how the program is going from their perspective. We will also continue to monitor weight, BMI, and behavioral health checks with the students. We will use the information from the staff and students/parents to determine if any part of the program needs modification, or if a change occurred, also known as outcome-focused empowerment evaluation (Yuen et. al, 2009). Empowerment evaluations will give our staff the space to reflect on how this program is meeting the needs of the students and their role in the program. Both outcome and empowerment evaluations will provide our program with the necessary feedback to measure if our services appropriately address the need. To help determine if change has occurred, we aim to answer the following questions:

- Are milestones and timelines being met?
- Are the objectives as stated truly measurable?
- Are changes necessary?
- Are program refinements possible?
- Is the program on track to meet goals?

Looking at the objectives for the program that consist of increasing the students and their families' knowledge of healthy foods and incorporating a healthy exercise routine, we anticipate reaching our desired milestones by a 50% increase. This would indicate that students are aware of the foods they consume, and that exercise can help maintain a healthy body weight.

Milestones will be measured by the information collected through student journals and feedback from their parents. Hopefully, BMI and weight measurements, along with feedback from staff, will demonstrate the need to provide more fruits and vegetables during lunch and snack breaks. As meal plan applications are utilized, we can gauge the family's support for their child.

Although we expect to see major changes in our students and their families' eating and physical activities, we cannot ignore the possibility of modifications that may be needed for the program to improve.

One of the aspects that we may want to consider for future changes in our evaluation plans is hiring an outside evaluator. We would consider this alternative to using internal staff because the large amount of information that needs to be processed and the extensive amount of time needed to analyze all the data can be overwhelming to the staff. Hiring an experienced outside evaluator will give us an unbiased opinion of how our program could better serve the community as well as tell us what we need to improve on from an outsider's perspective.

Collecting sample data at the start of the program would help to determine the best questionnaire and survey questions to ask students to help them express their thoughts and provide more detailed information that can be useful in the evaluation process. Lastly, utilizing focus groups more to collect information may possibly benefit the program because most kids feel more comfortable giving information or discussing information in groups with their peers.

Considering the potential increase in testing scores, utilization use from the meal plan app, increase physical activities among the students according to their journal and surveys, and lower BMI/waist measurement, we are showing that we are on track to meet our goals.

Summative Evaluation: After Program Activity

Through the continuous process of administrating the same survey questions to the students, parents, guardians, and school staff, the questions will be phased differently, and we will analyze the results from a qualitative perspective. The multiple choice and scale range surveys along with the mid-program BMI and weight scores will give us qualitative data or measurable data to see if the educational sessions are benefiting the students. Lower weight changes and indications through surveys of a healthier diet and positive responses to the program will indicate that we are on the right track to optimal health. An opposite result, of course, will prompt us to adjust the program. Adjustments may be in the form of increasing sessions in one area, such as physical activity and decreasing nutritional sessions or changing the specific program activities based on the student's needs. To help determine this we aim to answer the following questions:

- Did the program meet the outcome?
- Did the outcome support the objectives?
- Did the program reach a natural end of life?
- What could have been done differently?

With an increase of the meal plan app, physical activity, and test scores from the program, we hope to meet the anticipated outcome. In a retrospective plan, we foresee that the students' consumption of fruit and vegetable intake will increase considerably along with their exercise regimens during and outside the school program. Our program demonstrates the overall objective of providing a food program that works with the community to address obesity and unhealthy eating habits. We predict that through increased usage of the meal plan app and survey results, the program will not reach the end of life because we plan to project a two–to three-year span of the program. In requesting a two-year grant, we can consistently continue with the program's goals and objectives without any unexpected breaks. This will also help to retain the information the students learn and encourage them to continue practicing healthy habits. In the future, we hope to provide a more convenient method to collect and analyze data through computerized programs and Artificial Intelligence tools.

In conclusion, *Smart Moves: Bunche Edition* is more than just an after-school program; it is a meaningful step toward health equality for children and families in underserved communities such as Compton. By addressing the root causes of childhood obesity through education, emotional wellness, physical activity, and family engagement, this initiative creates opportunities for lasting change. Grounded in research and shaped by the voices of the community, this program is designed to meet kids where they are and support them every step of the way. With the support of funding, we can truly bring this vision to fruition, helping children build healthier habits, supporting families in making positive changes, and laying the groundwork for a stronger, more equitable future.

References

** References excluded for saving space **

Appendix 1: Logic Model

INPUTS	ACTIVITIES	OUTPUTS	OUTCOMES	IMPACTS
• Program space via Bunche Middle School
• Personnel fees: Program Coordinator, Registered Dietician, Mental Health Professional, Trained Physiologist
• Fitness and AV equipment
• Room supplies and educational materials (brochures and pamphlets)
• Healthy food/snacks and drinks	• Health and wellness education sessions
• Mental health counseling for food relationship and behaviors
• Physical activities including sports, dance, and a variety of cardiovascular activities
• Nutritional supp and education	• 24 sessions of physical activity with Trained Physiologists
• 12 sessions of nutritional education with Registered Dieticians
• 12 sessions of behavioral counseling with Mental Health Professionals
• 100-200 students/participants actively engaged in fitness curriculum
• 100-200 marketing resources
• 3,500 snacks for students/participants	• 60% of families (students, parents, caregivers) will report the use of meal planning apps, schedule of daily physical activity, and reading of nutrition labels
• 40% of participants will self-report continued healthy eating and physical activity habits and maintain or improve their overall BMI
• 20% of participants will increase their physical activity by 2x/week
• 15% of participants will practice mindful eating and less emotional eating	• After 2-3 years, 70% of students and parents will score at least 20% or more on a post program quiz assessing their knowledge on healthier food and physical activities
• 45% of students will continue with their learnings and submit weekly journals for review
• 40% of students and participants report an increase in consumption of fruits, vegetables, whole grains, and a reduction in sugary snacks and beverages

Appendix 2: Sources and Uses Budget

Smart Moves - Bunche Edition
Sources and Uses Budget

		RWJ	HTP	LADF	TOTAL
Personnel					
	Program Coordinator	$ 9,600	$ 9,600		$9,600
	Physiologist (Trainers)	$ 11,520		$ 11,520	$11,520
	Registered Dietician/Nutritionist	$ 13,440		$ 13,440	$13,440
	Mental Health Professional	$ 13,440		$ 13,440	$13,440
Benefits @ 30%		$14,400	$ 2,880	$ 11,520	$14,400
	TOTAL SALARY & BENEFITS	$62,400	0 $ 12,480	$ 49,920	$ 62,400
Operating Expenses					
	Facility Lease	$ 4,500	$ 4,500		$ 4,500
	Equipment & Supplies	$ 5,000	$ 5,000		$ 5,000
	Food/Drinks	$ 6,500	$ 6,500		$ 6,500
	Marketing Materials	$ 1,500	$ 1,500		$ 1,500
	TOTAL DIRECT COSTS	$ 79,900	$ 11,500 $ 18,480	0	$ 79,900
Indirect Cost @ 10%		$ 7,990	$ 5,000 $ 2,500	490	$ 7,990
TOTAL		$ 87,890	$ 16,500 $ 20,980	$ 50,410	$ 87,890

Appendix 3: Budget Narrative/Justification

Personnel Budget Justification as referenced in Appendix 2: Sources and Uses Budget.

- Program Coordinator - 1 FTE @ $9,600. Two half-time Program Coordinators will be responsible for enrolling students and maintaining records of the Smart Moves Bunch Program. They will supervise the staff and volunteers to ensure that each nutritional session, physical activity, and mental health session run smoothly and provide information to families.

- Trained Physiologists - 1 FTE @ $11,520. Two half-time trainers will facilitate the physical activity workshops for our students/participants and provide them the subject matter learnings for the students to succeed.

- Registered Dietician/Nutritionist - 1 FTE @ $13,440. Two half-time dieticians will facilitate the nutritional education workshops for students and families to educate on healthy food choices and nutrition labels.

- Mental Health Professional - 1 FTE @ $13,440. Two half-time dieticians will facilitate behavioral education and counseling for participants to focus on their food relationship habits.

Benefits Budget Justification: As referenced in Appendix 2: Sources and Uses Budget

- Calculated at 30% and includes health and dental insurance, and mandatory benefits that include Social Security Income, worker's compensations, FICA and others.

Operating Expenses Budget Justification: As referenced in Appendix 2: Sources and Uses Budget

- Facility Lease – @ $4,500. Leasing cost provided to the middle school for using their auditorium, gymnasium and resources for the

Smart Moves workshops and activities to take place, throughout the course of the program.

- Equipment and Supplies – @ $5,000. For the purchase of exercise equipment for cardio, like bicycles and treadmills along with sports equipment like balls, flags for football that will be used during the physical activity workshops. Part of this budget will also go to providing our registered dieticians and mental health professionals with funds for workspace furniture for their nutrition session and mental health counseling.

- Food and Drinks - @ $6,500. To provide our students and participants with healthy snacks and beverages, for both nutrition and education over the course of the program.

- Marketing Materials - @ $1,500. Costs associated with advertisement and printed education materials for students and their families.

- Indirect Costs – Based on a provisional cost rate of 10%.

Glossary

- **Abstract (Proposal):** A concise, factual summary of a grant proposal's core components (goals, methods, expected outcomes), typically one paragraph, designed for quick reference and indexing, not persuasion.

- **Accountability (Evaluation):** The obligation to demonstrate and justify the use of resources and the achievement of results to stakeholders, including funders, beneficiaries, and the public, often evidenced through evaluation findings.

- **Accountable Stewardship:** The ethical and financial responsibility of an organization to manage grant funds transparently and effectively, ensuring resources are used as promised and impacts are measured and reported.

- **Activities (Program):** The specific actions, services, or interventions a program undertakes to achieve its objectives and deliver its intended benefits.

- **Active Voice:** A grammatical construction where the subject of a sentence performs the action of the verb (e.g., "We will implement the program"), generally preferred in grant writing for clarity, directness, and impact.

- **Advocacy (Grant Writing):** The act of using a grant proposal as a persuasive tool to make a compelling case for an organization's mission and needs, articulating why a community or cause matters and deserves resources.

- **Allowable Costs:** Expenses that a funder permits to be charged to a grant, as defined by their specific guidelines, regulations (e.g., OMB Uniform Guidance for federal grants), and the terms of the grant agreement.

- **Analytical Insight:** The ability to gain a deep and clear understanding of complex information or situations by systematically breaking them down and examining their constituent components, as applied in proposal analysis.

- **Audit (Grant):** A formal, independent examination of an organization's financial records and grant-related activities to ensure compliance with the terms of the grant agreement, applicable regulations, and accounting standards.

- **Authorized Organizational Representative (AOR):** An individual formally designated and authorized by an organization to submit grant applications, sign grant agreements, and enter into legal obligations on behalf of the organization, particularly for federal grants.

- **Authorship (Grant Proposal):** The act or fact of originating the content of a grant proposal, particularly relevant in collaborative efforts or when external writers are involved, emphasizing clear responsibility for the submitted text.

- **Baseline Data:** Data collected at the beginning of a program or before an intervention is implemented, serving as a point of comparison to measure changes, progress, or impact over time.

- **Benchmarks (Evaluation):** Quantifiable thresholds or specific targets that a program aims to achieve for each indicator, signaling successful progress towards goals or the attainment of objectives.

- **Budget (Grant):** A detailed financial plan outlining all anticipated revenues and expenditures for a proposed project or program, serving as a blueprint that demonstrates financial accountability, resource management, and programmatic feasibility.

- **Budget-to-Actuals Report:** A financial report that compares the actual expenditures and revenues of a program or organization against its approved budget for a specific period, highlighting any variances and requiring explanations for significant differences.

- **Budget Narrative:** A written explanation that complements the numeric budget, detailing the rationale, calculation, and purpose behind each proposed expense, ensuring transparency and alignment with program activities.

- **Capital Budget:** A financial plan that specifically details proposed expenditures for major, long-term investments in physical assets such as infrastructure, facility improvements, land acquisition, or large equipment purchases, often having a significant cost and an extended useful life.

- **Cash Flow Management (Grant):** The process of monitoring, analyzing, and optimizing the movement of cash into and out of an organization or a specific grant-funded project, crucial for maintaining liquidity, especially with reimbursement-based grants.

- **Causality (Evaluation):** The relationship where one event or action (the program intervention) is directly responsible for causing another event or outcome; establishing strong causality is often the goal of rigorous evaluation designs.

- **Candid:** A nonprofit organization that provides data, research, and tools (like Foundation Directory Online) to support the philanthropic sector, helping grantseekers find funding and understand funders.

- **Clean Hands: Brighter and Healthier Future (Sample Proposal):** A hypothetical grant proposal examined in this book, outlining a school-based hand hygiene education pilot program.

- **Coherence (Proposal Writing):** The quality of a grant proposal where all sections and ideas are logically connected, flow smoothly, and consistently contribute to a unified, persuasive message, without internal contradictions or abrupt shifts.

- **Common Pitfalls (Grant Writing):** Frequent mistakes or challenges encountered during any stage of grant proposal development or management, which can lead to inefficiencies, rejections, or implementation issues.

- **Community and Stakeholder Support:** The engagement and endorsement from individuals or groups who will be affected by or are essential to a project's success, including beneficiaries, partners, and community leaders.

- **Community Foundation:** A public charity that pools philanthropic resources from multiple donors to serve a specific geographic area, making grants that address local needs and priorities.

- **Comparison Group:** A group of individuals or entities that is similar to the program's participants but does not receive the intervention, used in some evaluation designs (e.g., quasi-experimental) to help attribute observed outcomes to the program.

- **Compliance (Grant):** Adherence to all the specific terms, conditions, regulations, and guidelines stipulated in a grant agreement, funder policies, and applicable local, state, or federal laws.

- **Conciseness:** The quality of writing clearly and effectively using no more words than are necessary, crucial for grant proposals with strict word or page limits, enhancing clarity and impact.

- **Confidentiality (Evaluation):** The ethical principle of protecting the privacy of program participants' identities and personal information gathered during evaluation activities, ensuring data is not shared inappropriately.

- **Conflicts of Interest (Grant Writing):** Situations where an individual's or organization's personal, financial, or professional interests could potentially compromise, or appear to compromise, their objectivity, integrity, or fairness in grant seeking or consulting engagements.

- **Contingency Planning (Grant):** The process of developing alternative strategies or backup plans within a grant proposal or management process to address potential unforeseen challenges, delays, or changes that could impact project implementation or outcomes.

- **Continuous Quality Improvement (CQI):** A management philosophy and systematic approach that uses data and iterative cycles of planning, doing, studying, and acting (PDSA) to continuously enhance the quality, efficiency, and effectiveness of programs and processes.

- **Corporate Foundation:** A legally separate nonprofit entity established and funded by a corporation, making grants in line with its own board-governed priorities, often aligning with the parent company's values.

- **Corporate Giving Programs (CSR Programs):** Philanthropic initiatives operated directly by a corporation (not a separate foundation), which may include direct cash gifts, in-kind donations, or employee matching gift programs, often tied to corporate social responsibility goals.

- **Cost-Benefit Analysis:** An evaluation method that assigns a monetary value to both the costs of a program and its anticipated or realized benefits (monetized) to determine if the benefits outweigh the costs, providing an economic justification for the investment.

- **Cost-Effectiveness Analysis:** An evaluation method that compares the costs of a program to its achieved outcomes, without necessarily monetizing the outcomes, to determine the most efficient way to achieve a specific result (e.g., cost per outcome achieved).

- **Cost-Sharing and Matching Funds:** Contributions (cash or in-kind) from the applicant organization or partner organizations that supplement the requested grant funds, demonstrating buy-in, leveraging the funder's investment, and expanding total project resources.

- **Cost Centers (Accounting):** Distinct units, departments, or individual programs within an organization for which costs are separately tracked, managed, and reported, often used for individual grant-funded projects to facilitate fiscal oversight.

- **Council on Foundations:** An association that supports and promotes philanthropy, serving as a voice for family, community, and corporate foundations, and advocating for policies that strengthen the sector.

- **Data Collection Tools:** Instruments or methods used to gather information for evaluation, such as surveys, questionnaires, interview guides, focus group protocols, observation checklists, or standardized assessments.

- **Data Security (Evaluation):** The measures taken to protect sensitive information collected during evaluation from unauthorized access, use, disclosure, disruption, modification, or destruction, ensuring ethical data management.

- **Deliverables (Grant):** The specific, tangible products, services, or outcomes that an organization is contractually obligated to provide or achieve as part of a grant agreement, representing the concrete outputs of the project.

- **Developmental Evaluation:** An evaluation approach conducted during the early stages of concept development for innovative, complex, or rapidly evolving programs, providing real-time feedback to help shape and adapt the program as it emerges.

- **Documentation and Recordkeeping (Grant):** The meticulous practice of maintaining comprehensive written and digital records (e.g., receipts, invoices, timesheets, communications, reports) related to a grant, essential for financial oversight, reporting, and audit readiness.

- **Equity-Focused Giving (DEI):** Grantmaking strategies that explicitly prioritize Diversity, Equity, and Inclusion (DEI) by supporting organizations and initiatives that address systemic disparities, particularly those led by or serving historically marginalized communities.

- **Ethical Breaches (Grant Writing):** Violations of professional standards of conduct, honesty, or integrity in the grant writing process, such as misrepresentation, plagiarism (including uncritical reuse), or misuse of confidential information.

- **Ethical Budgeting:** The practice of preparing a grant budget with complete transparency, accuracy, and honesty, ensuring that all costs are justifiable, realistic, and directly aligned with proposed activities and funder guidelines, avoiding inflation or hidden expenses.

- **Evaluation Plan:** A systematic roadmap outlining how a program's progress and effectiveness will be measured, including its purpose, questions, methodology, indicators, data collection methods, timeline, and assigned roles.

- **Evaluation Questions:** Specific, clear, and answerable questions that an evaluation is designed to address, directly linked to program goals and objectives, guiding the entire evaluation process.

- **Executive Summary (Proposal):** A persuasive and comprehensive overview of an entire grant proposal, designed to capture attention, articulate the project's significance, and compel the funder to review the full proposal.

- **Experimental Design (RCT):** A rigorous evaluation methodology (often a Randomized Controlled Trial) that involves randomly assigning participants to a treatment group (receives intervention) and a control group (does not) to establish strong evidence of causality between an intervention and observed outcomes.

- **External Evaluator:** An independent professional or firm hired from outside the organization to conduct an evaluation, often bringing objectivity, specialized expertise, and enhanced credibility to the findings.

- **Feasibility Study (Grant):** An internal assessment conducted before writing a grant proposal to determine an organization's readiness and capacity to successfully plan, implement, and sustain a proposed project.

- **Fidelity (Program Implementation):** The degree to which a program is implemented exactly as it was originally designed and intended, ensuring adherence to its core components, activities, and protocols.

- **Fiscal Health (Organization):** An organization's financial stability, sound management practices, and capacity to responsibly manage funds, often demonstrated through financial statements and audit reports.

- **Fiscal Oversight (Grant):** The continuous monitoring and management of financial resources for a grant-funded project, ensuring that funds are spent appropriately, tracked accurately, reported transparently, and adhere to budget and compliance requirements.

- **Formative Evaluation:** An evaluation conducted *during* a program's active implementation, providing ongoing, real-time feedback for mid-course corrections, process improvement, and optimization of program delivery.

- **Foundations:** Legal entities established and funded to distribute financial grants to organizations or individuals for charitable, scientific, cultural, educational, or other public benefit purposes.

- **Funder Fit:** The degree to which a proposed project aligns with a specific funder's stated priorities, geographic focus, and typical funding scale, indicating a strong potential match.

- **Funder Language Alignment:** The strategic practice of mirroring the specific terminology, phrasing, values, and priorities used by a funder in their guidelines, mission statement, or recent grantmaking, to demonstrate strong organizational fit.

- **Functional Budget:** A budget format that organizes costs by the specific program function, activity, or organizational component they support (e.g., direct service delivery, outreach, evaluation), often used for complex projects with multiple distinct operational areas.

- **Ghostwriting (Grant):** The practice of writing a grant proposal, or significant portions of it, for an organization without being publicly credited as the author, which necessitates robust internal systems to ensure the content genuinely reflects the organization's true voice and capacity.

- **Goals (Program):** Broad, aspirational statements that describe the desired long-term change a program aims to achieve, serving as its ultimate vision.

- **Grant Agreement:** A legally binding contract between a funder and a grantee that formally outlines the terms, conditions, deliverables, approved budget, reporting schedule, and compliance requirements for an awarded grant.

- **Grant Closeout:** The final phase of the grant lifecycle, involving the completion and submission of all final reports, financial reconciliation, asset disposition, and archiving of records once the grant period ends.

- **Grant Funding Landscape:** The overall environment of grantmaking, including its competitive nature, the types of funders, their priorities, and the trends influencing philanthropic giving.

- **Grant Management (Post-Award):** All activities undertaken by a grantee organization after a grant has been awarded, encompassing financial management, program implementation oversight, ongoing communication with the funder, and compliance with grant terms.
- **Grant Proposal:** A formal, written request for financial or in-kind support, submitted to a funder by an organization seeking resources for a specific project or program.
- **Grants.gov:** The centralized online portal for U.S. federal grant opportunities, providing a single access point for organizations to find and apply for federal funding.
- **Impact Evaluation:** An evaluation that attempts to determine whether a program caused or significantly contributed to long-term, broader changes in the target population, community, or system, often at a societal level.
- **Impacts (Program):** The long-term, broader changes or improvements to which a program contributes, often extending beyond the grant period and influencing systemic shifts at a community or societal level.
- **Implementation Plan:** A detailed schedule or work plan outlining the sequence of activities, timelines, and assigned responsibilities for putting a program into action.
- **Indicators (Evaluation):** Specific, observable, and measurable signs or metrics that demonstrate whether a program is progressing as planned or achieving its intended changes (e.g., a percentage increase, a reduction in incidents).
- **Individual Development Plan (IDP):** (From Chapter 5 example, not a core term to define unless explicitly requested. Skipping for now.)
- **Industrial Capitalism:** (Historical term from Chapter 1, not core grant term, skipping for now.)

- **Integrity (Grant Writing):** The unwavering adherence to strong moral and ethical principles throughout the entire grant seeking and management process, encompassing honesty, transparency, consistency between promises and actions, and a commitment to responsible stewardship.

- **Informed Consent (Evaluation):** The ethical principle of ensuring that participants in an evaluation fully understand the purpose, procedures, potential risks, and benefits of their involvement before voluntarily agreeing to participate.

- **Inputs (Logic Model):** The resources invested in a program (e.g., funding, staff time, volunteer contributions, equipment, facilities, materials) that are necessary to carry out its planned activities.

- **Internal Debrief (Grant):** A meeting held within an organization, often at the close of a grant or project, to review successes, challenges, lessons learned, and recommendations for future programs and grant strategies, fostering institutional knowledge.

- **Internal Evaluator:** An evaluator who is a staff member within the organization implementing the program, offering deep institutional knowledge, ongoing accessibility, and fostering internal learning and capacity building.

- **Inverse Outlining:** A revision technique where an outline is created *from* an existing draft (rather than before drafting) to assess its logical flow, coherence, argument structure, and overall organization.

- **Invoice (Grant):** A formal request for payment submitted to a funder, typically used for reimbursement of expenses already incurred by the grantee, as per the payment schedule outlined in the grant agreement.

- **Jargon:** Specialized or technical words and phrases used by a particular profession, group, or field that may be difficult for a general audience to understand; to be avoided in grant proposals unless explicitly appropriate for the funder.

- **Key Performance Indicator (KPI):** (Used in Chapter 5 examples. Good to add.)

- **Kickoff Strategy (Grant):** A structured internal process initiated at the beginning of proposal development to align the grant team, distribute funder guidelines, set timelines, and clearly assign tasks.

- **Letter of Inquiry (LOI):** A preliminary, brief letter sent to a funder to gauge their interest in a project idea before submitting a full grant proposal, often a required first step.

- **Line Item Budget:** A budget format that lists expenses by specific, detailed categories (e.g., personnel salaries, office supplies, travel expenses) with individual allocated amounts, valued for its clarity and simplicity in tracking expenditures.

- **Logic Model:** A visual representation of a program's theory of change, illustrating the causal links between its inputs (resources), activities, outputs, short-term outcomes, and long-term impacts.

- **Memorandum of Understanding (MOU):** A formal, non-binding agreement between two or more parties that outlines their shared understanding, roles, and responsibilities for a collaborative project or partnership.

- **Misrepresentation (Grant Proposal):** The act of providing inaccurate, misleading, or exaggerated information in a grant proposal, either intentionally or unintentionally, which can damage an organization's credibility and lead to severe consequences.

- **Mixed Methods (Evaluation):** An evaluation approach that systematically combines both quantitative and qualitative data collection and analysis methods within a single study to provide a more comprehensive and nuanced understanding of program effectiveness and impact.

- **No-Cost Extension (NCE):** A formal request submitted to a funder to extend the grant period beyond its original end date without requesting additional funding, usually granted to allow more time to complete project activities or expend remaining funds.

- **Notices of Funding Opportunities (NOFOs):** Formal announcements from government agencies (especially federal) detailing available grant funding, eligibility requirements, application instructions, and programmatic priorities.

- **Objectives (Program):** Specific, measurable, achievable, relevant, and time-bound (SMART) steps that directly lead toward a program's broader goal, forming the backbone of project planning and evaluation.

- **Observation (Qualitative Method):** A systematic method of collecting data by watching and recording behaviors, interactions, or events in a program setting, which can be structured or unstructured.

- **OMB Uniform Guidance (2 CFR Part 200):** A comprehensive set of federal regulations (Office of Management and Budget Uniform Administrative Requirements, Cost Principles, and Audit Requirements for Federal Awards) that establishes consistent standards for all federal awards to non-federal entities.

- **Operating Foundation:** A type of foundation that uses most of its income and resources to directly run its own charitable programs or initiatives, rather than primarily making grants to outside organizations.

- **Organizational Capacity (Grant):** The internal resources (staffing, infrastructure, leadership support, financial systems, expertise) an organization possesses to successfully plan, implement, and manage a grant-funded program.

- **Organizational Chart:** A visual representation of an organization's internal structure, showing reporting relationships, departments, and the hierarchy of positions.

- **Outcomes (Program):** The immediate and intermediate changes or benefits (e.g., in knowledge, attitudes, skills, behaviors, or conditions) that result directly from program activities for participants or systems.

- **Outcomes-Based Evaluation:** An evaluation design that specifically focuses on measuring the short-term, intermediate, or long-term changes (outcomes) that result directly from a program's activities in its target population or system.

- **Overpromising (Grant Proposal):** An ethical misstep in grant writing where an organization commits to achieving more outcomes or impacts than is realistically possible given its genuine capacity, available resources, or proposed timeline, potentially leading to failure in implementation.

- **Parallel Construction:** A writing technique that uses similar grammatical forms or structures to express ideas of equal importance (e.g., in a list or series), enhancing readability, professionalism, and emphasizing the balance of points.

- **Participatory Evaluation:** An approach to evaluation that actively involves program stakeholders and beneficiaries in the design, conduct, and interpretation of the evaluation, fostering ownership, relevance, and utilization of findings.

- **Passive Voice:** A grammatical construction where the subject of a sentence receives the action of the verb (e.g., "The program was implemented by our team"), often making writing less direct, clear, and impactful than active voice.

- **Peer or Expert Review (Proposal):** A crucial stage in the revision process where a draft grant proposal is assessed by knowledgeable colleagues, subject matter experts, or professional grant writers to provide feedback, identify weaknesses, and ensure quality before submission.

- **Performance-Based Budget:** A budgeting model where funding allocations or disbursements are explicitly tied to the achievement of specific, measurable milestones or predetermined outcomes, emphasizing results over mere expenditures.

- **Philanthropic Environment:** The broader context of giving, encompassing the various types of funders, their historical roots, legal structures, motivations, and current trends in grantmaking.

- **Philanthropy:** The practice of using personal wealth or resources for public good; derived from the Greek for "love of mankind," evolving from spontaneous giving to structured, mission-driven social investment.

- **Plain Language:** Writing that is clear, concise, well-organized, and easy for the target audience to understand, avoiding jargon, overly complex sentence structures, and unnecessary wordiness.

- **Post-Award Management:** (See Grant Management (Post-Award)) - *Self-correction: Will ensure this points to the main term.*

- **Preface (Book):** A section at the beginning of a book, written by the author, explaining the motivation for writing the book, its scope, and often including personal reflections and acknowledgments.

- **Private Foundation:** A legal entity typically funded by a single individual, family, or corporation, making grants from an endowment to other organizations or individuals for charitable purposes.

- **Process-Based Evaluation:** An evaluation design that examines *how* a program was implemented, assessing aspects such as fidelity to the proposed model, the quality of service delivery, operational efficiency, and participant engagement.

- **Program Description:** The section of a grant proposal that comprehensively explains what a program intends to do, how it will be implemented, and why its chosen methods are the most effective in addressing the identified need.

- **Program Improvement:** The ongoing process of refining and enhancing program design and service delivery based on data, feedback, and evaluation findings, aiming for increased effectiveness.

- **Program Officer:** A professional staff member at a grantmaking organization (foundation, corporation, government agency) responsible for managing a portfolio of grants, reviewing proposals, and maintaining relationships with grantees.

- **Proofreading:** The final, meticulous stage of revision focused specifically on catching mechanical errors such as typos, punctuation mistakes, grammatical errors, and formatting inconsistencies before final submission.

- **Public Foundations:** Organizations that raise funds from the general public (e.g., through individual donations) and often focus on specific missions, sometimes operating their own programs alongside grantmaking.

- **Qualitative Evidence:** Non-numerical data (e.g., client stories, testimonials, expert opinions, focus group insights, observations) used to provide depth, context, and human impact to a problem or program.

- **Qualitative Methods (Evaluation):** Evaluation approaches that rely on non-numerical data (e.g., in-depth interviews, focus groups, observations, case studies) to capture experiences, perspectives, meanings, and provide rich contextual understanding.

- **Quantitative Evidence:** Measurable, numerical data and statistics (e.g., percentages, numbers, trends, rates) used to define the scope and urgency of a problem or to quantify program activities and outcomes.

- **Quantitative Methods (Evaluation):** Evaluation approaches that rely on measurable, numerical data (e.g., surveys with scaled responses, statistics, performance tracking) to quantify findings, identify trends, and make statistical comparisons.

- **Quasi-Experimental Design:** An evaluation methodology similar to an experimental design but without random assignment of participants, typically using comparison groups or other methods to infer causality, though with greater caveats than a true experiment.

- **Recycling Proposals (Uncritical Reuse):** The practice of reusing significant portions of a previously written grant proposal for a new application without meticulously tailoring the content to the new funder's unique priorities, guidelines, or specific context, which can be misleading and unprofessional.

- **Reliability (Evaluation):** The consistency or dependability of a measurement tool or method; if repeated under the same conditions, would it yield similar results?

- **Reimbursement-Based Grant:** A type of grant funding where the grantee first expends its own funds on approved activities and then submits documentation to the funder to request repayment, as opposed to receiving funds upfront.

- **Reporting (Grant):** The periodic submission of narrative, financial, and evaluation updates to a funder, detailing program progress, expenditures, challenges, and outcomes as required by the grant agreement and funder policies.

- **Request for Proposals (RFP):** Detailed documents issued by funders (often government agencies or large foundations) that solicit formal proposals for specific projects, outlining requirements, scope of work, and evaluation criteria.

- **Revenue and Expense Budget:** A financial plan that includes both projected income (revenue from all sources) and projected expenditures for a specific period (e.g., a fiscal year or the grant period), offering a comprehensive overview of financial operations.

- **Revision Process (Proposal):** An iterative, multi-stage process of reviewing and refining a grant proposal for its content, structure, language, and mechanics to ensure its clarity, persuasiveness, professionalism, and adherence to funder requirements.

- **Rigorous Logic (Program Design):** The quality of a program's underlying design and its theory of change being sound, well-reasoned, and demonstrating clear, defensible cause-and-effect relationships from activities to intended outcomes and impacts.

- **Root Causes:** The underlying, systemic, or situational factors that contribute to a problem, moving beyond its surface-level symptoms to identify deeper origins.

- **SAM.gov:** The System for Award Management, a U.S. federal government website used for registering entities that wish to do business with the U.S. government, including applying for and receiving federal grants.

- **Scope Changes (Grant):** Any significant alteration to the proposed project's activities, objectives, target population, or budget from what was originally approved in the grant agreement, typically requiring formal funder approval.

- **Self-Citation (Academic Context):** In academic publishing, the formal practice of citing one's own previous work when reusing material, even when the author is the sole originator of both works, emphasizing attribution and academic integrity.

- **Seamless Reading Experience:** The quality of a grant proposal or any manuscript where the text flows smoothly, logically, and coherently from one section or idea to the next, without abrupt shifts, jargon, or inconsistencies that disrupt the reader's comprehension.

- **"Show, Don't Just Tell":** A powerful writing principle that advises demonstrating a concept, claim, or impact with concrete evidence, specific data, vivid examples, or compelling anecdotes, rather than simply stating it as a general fact.

- **Smart Moves: Bunche Edition (Sample Proposal):** A hypothetical grant proposal examined in this book, outlining an equity-focused after-school program to address childhood obesity.

- **Social Impact Investing:** A financial model that deploys capital (e.g., loans, equity) to generate both a financial return and a measurable positive social or environmental impact, blurring the lines between traditional investment and philanthropy.

- **Sources and Uses Budget:** A comprehensive financial budget format that clearly delineates all anticipated sources of revenue (grants, matching funds, in-kind) and how every dollar will be spent (uses), ensuring that total sources equal total uses.

- **Statement of Need:** The section of a grant proposal that uses compelling data, evidence, and narrative to define a problem, articulate its urgency, demonstrate its solvability, and convince the funder of the organization's deep understanding of the issue.

- **Strategic Alignment (Grant):** The consistency of a proposed project with an organization's established mission, values, and long-term strategic goals, as well as its congruence with the specific priorities and mission of the potential funder.

- **Strategic Planning (Program):** The systematic process of defining a program's direction, making decisions on allocating its resources, and outlining actions to pursue its vision, achieve objectives, and contribute to overall organizational goals.

- **Strategic Storytelling (Grant Writing):** The art of transforming raw data and program plans into a clear, persuasive narrative that articulates a compelling need, presents an effective solution, and demonstrates anticipated impact, captivating a funder's attention.

- **Strategic Vision (Grant Writing):** A core philosophy in grant writing that emphasizes aligning a well-researched problem with a fundable solution, clearly tied to outcomes and funder priorities, often demonstrating foresight and planning.

- **Stretching the Truth (Grant Writing):** A colloquial term referring to the act of exaggerating claims, inflating needs or impacts, or otherwise presenting information in a grant proposal with less than full honesty, which ultimately erodes trust with funders.

- **Summative Evaluation:** An evaluation conducted at the conclusion of a program or funding period to assess its overall effectiveness, impact, and achievement of stated objectives, often used for accountability and major funding decisions.

- **Sustainability Plan:** A section within a grant proposal that outlines how a program or its positive impact will continue beyond the initial grant funding period, often involving diversified revenue streams or integration into core organizational operations.

- **Technical Assistance (Grant):** Specialized guidance, support, or consultation provided to grantseekers (e.g., during proposal development) or grantees (e.g., during program implementation or reporting) to enhance their capacity or address specific challenges.

- **Theory of Change Evaluation:** An evaluation approach that assesses the underlying assumptions and causal pathways articulated in a program's logic model, exploring whether the program's intended logic holds true in practice and identifying where the theory might break down.

- **Timelines (Program):** A schedule or work plan detailing the sequence, duration, and key milestones of a program's activities, often presented narratively within a proposal or as a visual chart in an appendix.

- **Topic Sentence:** The sentence that expresses the main idea or central purpose of a paragraph, often strategically placed at the beginning, guiding the reader through the argument.

- **Transitions (Writing):** Words, phrases, or sentences that smoothly connect ideas, paragraphs, or sections, ensuring a logical flow of thought and guiding the reader through the argument without abrupt shifts.

- **Transparency (Grant):** The principle of openness and clear communication in all aspects of grant seeking and management, including budgeting, reporting, and organizational practices, fostering trust and accountability with funders and stakeholders.

- **Triangulation (Evaluation):** The practice of using multiple data sources (e.g., surveys, interviews, administrative data), multiple methods (quantitative and qualitative), or multiple evaluators to corroborate findings and enhance the credibility, validity, and robustness of evaluation results.

- **Trust (Grantmaking):** The foundational element in funder-grantee relationships, built through consistent integrity, honest and proactive communication, demonstrated capability, and responsible stewardship of resources, leading to sustained partnerships.

- **Unallowable Costs:** Expenses that a funder explicitly prohibits from being charged to a grant, as defined by their guidelines or applicable regulations (e.g., lobbying, entertainment, fines).

- **Unique Entity Identifier (UEI):** A 12-character alphanumeric ID assigned to entities (such as organizations applying for federal grants) registered in SAM.gov, used by the U.S. federal government for identification and tracking purposes.

- **Utilization-Focused Evaluation:** An approach to evaluation emphasizing that the evaluation should be designed and conducted specifically to ensure its findings are genuinely used by specific, intended users to make decisions, prioritizing relevance and usability.

- **Validity (Evaluation):** The extent to which an evaluation accurately measures what it intends to measure, and whether its conclusions about program effectiveness or impact are sound, justifiable, and free from bias.

- **Variances (Budget):** The differences between actual expenditures and budgeted amounts in a financial report, often requiring detailed explanation if they are significant or fall outside permissible thresholds.

- **Venture Philanthropy:** A philanthropic model that borrows strategies from the business world, focusing on long-term investments in social enterprises, emphasizing metrics, scalability, and social return on investment.

- **Version Control (Documents):** A system or process for managing changes to documents over time, ensuring that the most current and accurate version of a proposal or report is identifiable and used, preventing errors in submission.

- **Whitespace (Formatting):** The empty space on a page or document, used strategically in design to improve readability, break up dense blocks of text, highlight important information, and provide visual relief.

- **Word/Page Limits:** Strict restrictions on the maximum number of words or pages allowed for a grant proposal or specific sections, requiring authors to be highly concise and prioritize content rigorously.

- **990 Finder:** Online tools (e.g., from ProPublica or Candid) that allow users to publicly access IRS Form 990s, revealing financial and grantmaking details of U.S. tax-exempt organizations, particularly foundations.

About the Author

David E. Fraser, Ed.D., MPA, is a highly respected scholar-practitioner, educator, and senior executive whose distinguished career spans over 30 years across government, higher education, and the nonprofit sector. His unique perspective is forged from direct experience: not only has he successfully secured over $25 million in grant funding, contracts, and philanthropic support for diverse public-sector initiatives and community nonprofits, but he has also meticulously evaluated countless proposals as a grant reviewer for agencies such as the **New York State Department of Health**, the **US Department of Housing & Urban Development (HUD) Region 9**, and **Contra Costa County's Keller Canyon Mitigation Fund**. This dual experience provides him with an unparalleled understanding of the grant lifecycle from both sides of the table.

As Chief of Staff to **two consecutive elected officials** in Contra Costa County for nearly two decades, Dr. Fraser has spearheaded legislative strategy, provided institutional oversight, and led substantial grant initiatives that have driven policy innovation, operational reform, and tangible community impact. His executive leadership roles also include significant contributions as Vice President of Programs at Volunteers of America, Bay Area, and senior positions with the City of Oakland, underscoring his deep commitment to public service and community development.

Dr. Fraser is an acclaimed academic who serves as a Graduate Faculty member at California State University, East Bay, within both the Master of Public Administration (MPA) and Master of Science in Healthcare Administration (MS-HCA) programs. He is the original architect of **HCA 642, a capstone course specifically focused on healthcare grant writing and program design**, where he imparts the practical strategies found within these pages. His Doctor of Education (Ed.D.) in Higher Education Leadership and a Master of Public Administration (MPA) provide a rigorous academic grounding, enabling him to bridge the worlds of scholarship and executive leadership. He further contributes to ethical, applied research as a full member of the university's Institutional Review Board (IRB).

Dr. Fraser's professional philosophy is characterized by strategic clarity, ethical leadership, and a profound respect for institutional mission—whether in government, higher education, or nonprofit administration. He thrives at the intersection of systems thinking and human impact, bringing a balanced perspective that is both scholarly and results-driven.

Through **Fraser Leadership Group**, he continues his dedication to advancing public service, institutional change, and cross-sector innovation, empowering leaders and driving meaningful outcomes.

www.ingramcontent.com/pod-product-compliance
Lightning Source LLC
Chambersburg PA
CBHW070616030426
42337CB00020B/3820